THE TOWER
PRESSURE COOK BOOK

Type 1—Tower Pressure Cooker

THE TOWER
PRESSURE COOK BOOK

by Annette Yates

W Foulsham & Co Ltd

London   New York   Toronto   Cape Town   Sydney

W. FOULSHAM & COMPANY LIMITED
Yeovil Road, Slough, Berkshire, SL1 4JH

ISBN 0-572-00970-4

The Publishers acknowledge with thanks the loan of
Pressure Cookers Types 2 and 3 by Prestige Group
Ltd and Tefal Housewares for photography and
testing purposes. Picture on page 32 by
kind permission of Empire Daities Ltd.

Designed by Peter Constable Ltd
Printed in Hong Kong by Colorcraft Ltd,

CONTENTS

Introduction	6
How to use your Pressure Cooker	7
Safety Note	10
How to care for your Pressure Cooker	11
Your Pressure Cooker and your Freezer	11
Advantages of pressure cooking	12
What about your Pressure Cooker	12
What you get	13
Soups and Starters	14
Meat	26
Poultry and Game	50
Fish	62
Vegetables	72
Desserts	82
All-in-one Meals	97
Entertaining	102
Preserves	108
Bottling	114
Weights and Measures	115
Index	117

Rating

Throughout the book the recipes have been given a rating.

 means the recipe is easy to prepare

 means the recipe needs a little special care during part or all of the preparation

means recipe is suitable for freezing.

INTRODUCTION

Whether you have just acquired a pressure cooker or have owned one for years, I hope it will give you as much pleasure as mine has given me. With each day we become more economy conscious and lead busier lives, so it is very satisfying to know that you and your pressure cooker can contribute to economizing on money, time and effort.

A pressure cooker is a useful piece of equipment for anyone to own. Whether you cook for one or two, for a sizable family, or for entertaining in large numbers, it makes sense to use a pressure cooker with all its cost-cutting advantages.

If you have a freezer, you will find your pressure cooker invaluable.

Do keep your pressure cooker handy for use. I have some friends who laid their pressure cooker to rest in a far corner of the cupboard once the initial excitement and interest had worn off. Like any other piece of kitchen equipment, it is used to its best advantage in conjunction with other equipment, such as the grill or the blender.

You will probably find, like me, that a timer clock is your pressure cooker's best friend. This will give you freedom to do other things while the pressure cooker is in use, without the risk of the food overcooking.

Don't forget to take the pressure cooker along on camping and caravan trips (and remember to take the timer). It is a great advantage when fuel is in short supply as well as when you wish to economize on fuel. You will also find that you have more time to appreciate your holiday.

I hope that you will enjoy trying the recipes in this book. With their help, basic and traditional meals, family ones and more exotic feasts can all be catered for.

Annette Yates

Type 2

How to use your pressure cooker

It is essential to follow the manufacturers' instructions for your particular model very carefully to obtain good results. When giving general instructions for use below, I have separated the main sorts of pressure cookers into types.

Type 1 has a pressure weight with an indicator plunger (Weight A, diagram p. 8).

Type 2 has a pressure weight consisting of fitted rings (Weight B, diagram p. 9).

Type 3 has a fixed $7\frac{1}{2}$-lb. pressure (diagram p.10).

TYPES 1 AND 2

1. Put the prepared food into the pressure cooker along with the accurate amount of liquid. Usually the minimum amount needed is $\frac{1}{2}$ pt/150 ml., but check the manufacturers' instructions to make sure. The quantity required will depend on the recipe being followed and the length of cooking time. The liquid used must always be one which gives off steam when it boils.

Remember to leave sufficient space above the food for steam to circulate or for foods to rise.
2. Place the lid in position, ensuring that it is firmly locked.
3. Place the pressure cooker on the heat.

TYPE 1

4. Place the indicator weight firmly in position on the central vent and turn the heat up full.
5. As the liquid boils, the pressure cooker fills with steam, some of which will be seen coming through the automatic air vent. This air vent will seal itself automatically, then the indicator plunger will rise as the pressure rises.
6. When the required pressure has been reached, shown by the number of silver rings, turn the heat down to maintain this pressure.

Time the cooking from now.

Type 3

TYPE 2

4. Place the correct weight firmly in position on the central vent. Turn the heat up full.

5. As the liquid boils, the pressure cooker fills with steam, expelling all the air. When the pressure builds up sufficiently inside the pressure cooker a slight hissing sound will be heard, followed by a much louder one as steam begins to escape. Do not leave the pressure cooker during this stage.

6. A continuous loud hissing indicates that pressure has now been reached, so turn down the heat until a continuous gentle 'muttering' is heard. This should be maintained throughout the cooking time.

Time the cooking from now.

TYPES 1 AND 2

7. At the end of the cooking time, remove the pressure cooker from the heat. Pressure must be reduced before removing the pressure weight or the lid. There are two methods of doing this:

TYPE 1

a. Reduce pressure slowly by allowing the pressure cooker to stand at room temperature, away from the heat, until the indicator plunger has dropped so no silver rings are visible, and the metal plunger in the automatic air vent has dropped to its normal position. The weight can now be lifted off and the lid removed.

TYPE 2

a. Reduce pressure slowly by allowing the pressure cooker to stand at room temperature, away from the heat. To test whether pressure has been reduced, lift the weight slightly. When no more steam escapes the weight can be lifted off and the lid removed.

TYPES 1 AND 2

This slower method should be used when: cooking liquid foods (such as soups and stews) and dried vegetables, all of which are liable to spurt out of the vent pipe on sudden reduction of pressure.

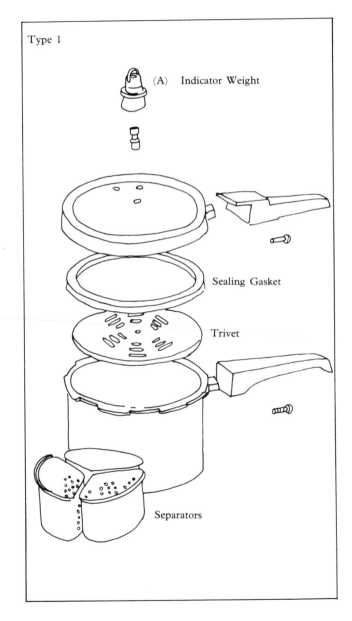

Type 1

(A) Indicator Weight

Sealing Gasket

Trivet

Separators

cooking egg custards and milk puddings which would curdle or separate with a sudden temperature drop,

cooking puddings containing a raising agent, which would sink with a sudden temperature drop, and bottling, where a sudden temperature drop would cause the jars to crack.

b.   Reduce pressure with cold water by standing the pressure cooker in a bowl of cold water.

This method should be used when the cooking time is vital. For example, vegetables would overcook if pressure was not reduced this way.

Note: Each recipe in this book indicates the correct method for reducing pressure.

TYPE 3

1.   Put the prepared food into the pressure cooker with the correct amount of liquid (refer to the manufacturers' instructions on the minimum quantity needed for particular recipes or methods of cooking). Remember that the liquid used must be one which gives off steam when it boils and do leave sufficient space above the food for steam to circulate or for foods to rise.

2.   Place the lid in position by sliding it on horizontally and fitting it carefully on to the rim of the pan. To tighten the lid, turn the knob in the direction of the arrow through two complete turns. The lid is now tight and locked.

3.   Position the rotating valve by placing it vertically on the vent on the lid and push down as far as it will go.

4.   Place the pressure cooker on the heat. As pressure is reached the valve begins to turn, emitting steam. *Time cooking from now.* Reduce the heat so that the valve remains still most of the time. A little steam will still be released, and the valve will occasionally turn slowly.

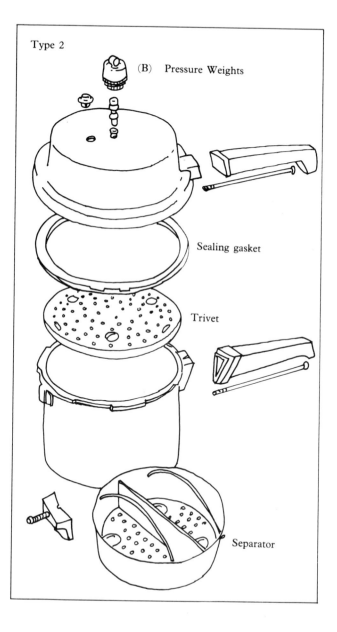

Type 2

(B)   Pressure Weights

Sealing gasket

Trivet

Separator

5.   At the end of the cooking time, remove the pressure cooker from the heat. Lower the pressure by lifting the rotating valve up to the first notch (do not remove it completely). This allows the steam to escape while the pressure falls. When all the steam has been expelled the lid can be removed. Do this by turning the knob in the opposite direction to the arrow until the clamp touches the lid. Lift the lid and slide it out horizontally.

If pressure is not reduced as soon as cooking is completed, the cooling steam condenses inside the pressure cooker, forming a vacuum and thus holding down the lid. If this should happen, reheat the pressure cooker for a few seconds with the knob in the open position. The lid will loosen itself.

Note: Since more steam is lost during cooking with pressure cooker Type 3 (cooking times will of course be longer than those for Types 1 and 2, as the cooking pressure is lower), more liquid is needed. In the following recipes, I have indicated where it is necessary to include extra liquid for this type of pressure cooker.

SAFETY

All pressure cookers include safety devices which operate if the vent pipe becomes blocked or if the pressure cooker boils dry and over-heats. Should the safety devices come into operation, the excess pressure is automatically released from the pressure cooker. However, if the manufacturers' instructions are carefully followed, the safety devices should never need to activate.

As a general rule, never fill the pressure cooker more than two-thirds full with solids or half-full with liquids or other foods that tend to boil over (for example, soups, milk, cereals, pastas). Sufficient space must always be left above the food for steam to circulate and for foods to rise.

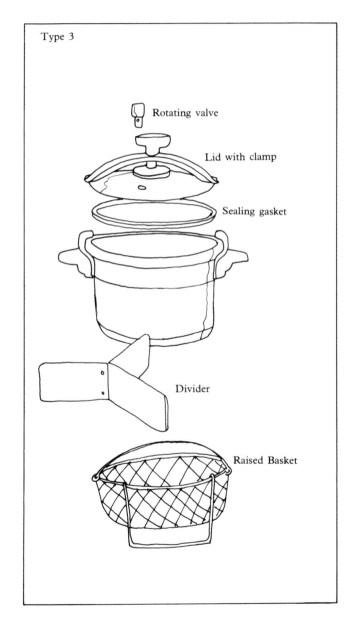

Type 3

Rotating valve

Lid with clamp

Sealing gasket

Divider

Raised Basket

How to care for your pressure cooker

Follow the manufacturers' instructions for washing and cleaning your pressure cooker, particularly those with non-stick interiors or coloured exteriors. Generally, the pressure cooker should be washed in warm soapy water, rinsed and dried. Discoloration inside the pressure cooker (usually seen when hard water is used for cooking) is harmless, but can easily be removed with soap pads, by cooking an acid fruit (such as cooking apples) in the pressure cooker, or by boiling up a strong solution of vinegar and water. When steaming puddings, add a little vinegar to the water to prevent such discoloration.

Washing soda should not be used to clean the pressure cooker, as this too causes discoloration.

Each time you use the pressure cooker check that the vent and the air vent are not blocked.

Before using a pressure cooker with a non-stick interior for the first time, wash it with hot soapy water, then rinse and dry it.

Do not use metal utensils or scouring pads on non-stick surfaces.

Handles, though heat-resistant, should not be left over direct heat.

All pressure cookers should be stored open to allow air circulation and to prevent the formation of musty smells. A neat way to store it is with the lid upside-down on the pressure-cooker base.

Finally, store your pressure cooker carefully. It is important that it should not be dented or its efficiency will be impaired. Do take care of the weights, particularly Weight A, which should not be immersed in water. Damage to the weight could cause malfunction.

Your pressure cooker and your freezer

Convenience is the key when you, your pressure cooker and your freezer get together. The pressure cooker can be used to prepare many foods and dishes for the freezer. Prepare larger quantities than normal, then eat some and freeze the rest.

When fruits are in season, prepare and freeze them for making jam, jelly or marmalade at a more convenient moment.

Vegetables can be blanched in a pressure cooker ready for freezing. It should be done at Medium/10-lb. pressure. Correct timing is absolutely vital. See page 72 for blanching times.

Most foods can be reheated in a pressure cooker straight from the freezer.

More details on using the pressure cooker in conjunction with the freezer appear in the introduction to each section, and instructions for freezing are given within the recipes where necessary.

Advantages of pressure cooking

Speed is the great advantage. Most foods can be cooked in one-third of their normal cooking time.

Since cooking times in a pressure cooker are so greatly reduced, considerable fuel savings are the obvious result. In addition, once the required pressure has been reached, only minimum heat is needed to maintain it. Even larger savings are made if more than one food is cooked at the same time. Try cooking some complete meals at once, for example.

In pressure-cooking, heat is forced through the food under pressure, tenderizing the food in the process. Thus, even the tougher (but flavoursome) cuts of meat are beautifully cooked in minutes rather than hours.

There is some loss of nutritive value in all methods of cooking. In a pressure cooker this loss is cut to a minimum by the short cooking times, the small amounts of liquids used and the exclusion of light and air.

Flavour is trapped inside the pressure cooker along with most of the cooking smells (some of which can be strong, or even undesirable).

Less steam escapes into the kitchen, and this can be quite an advantage when steaming puddings.

If a pressure cooker is used on camping or caravan trips, it will probably be the only piece of cooking equipment you will need to take.

Finally, a pressure cooker can be of great help when preparing food for special diets.

What about your pressure cooker

All pressure cookers work on the same principle, though there are several types and designs available. A pressure cooker is designed to trap and control the steam that normally escapes from an ordinary saucepan. This causes the pressure and temperature inside to increase gradually until it is automatically controlled by a weight or a valve system. It is this increase in pressure and temperature which causes the food to be cooked more quickly than by conventional methods, such as in the oven or on the cooker hob. Heat is literally forced through the food so that some cooking times are cut by as much as 75 per cent.

All pressure cookers can be used on any sort of fuel. They are usually made of pressed aluminium with polished exteriors, although some are available in stainless steel, others with a coloured finish and one with a non-stick interior.

There are various pressure cookers to choose from, and the most versatile offer three pressures: High/15-lb., Medium/10-lb. and Low/5-lb. Others offer two pressures: 15-lb. and 10-lb.

One operates at a fixed 15-lb. pressure and another at a fixed $7\frac{1}{2}$-lb. pressure. Most of these pressure cookers are also available in various sizes. When choosing a pressure cooker, the size that you choose will obviously depend on how much cooking you do and for how many people, but when deciding which type to buy the following guide to cooking under pressure may be useful.

High/15-lb. pressure is used for everyday cooking.

Medium/10-lb. pressure is used for softening fruit for jam, jelly and marmalade, and for bottling vegetables.

Low/5-lb. pressure is used for steaming mixtures containing raising agents and for bottling fruit.

What you get

Your pressure cooker consists of a pan with a tight-fitting lid. Between the lid and the pan is a flexible rubber gasket which ensures a tight seal under pressure. It is normally necessary to fix on the heat-resistant handles after purchase, and manufacturers' instructions for the particular model should be followed carefully.

TRIVET

This is a stand used when the food is to be cooked in steam and not in liquid. It is used, for example, with steamed puddings and pot roasts, but not for soups and stews where the food is cooked in the liquor and the flavours intermingle. It can also be used as a stand to separate layers of food. Some larger pressure cookers supply a set of legs to allow more space for food underneath the trivet, with the top layer lifted clear.

The trivet is used with the rim downward and is usually placed on top of the minimum amount of liquid required (refer to the manufacturers' instructions on this point). To lift the trivet out of the pressure cooker, hook a spoon or a fork into one of the slots.

SEPARATORS

Some models have two or three separators, perforated or unperforated. Others have just one separator with a divider. These are used to keep foods apart, preventing flavours from transferring from one food to another. They also enable the easy removal of food from the pressure cooker. The perforated separators are useful for cooking vegetables, the unperforated ones for stewing fruit, cooking rice and milk puddings, or for reheating portions of food.

The separators are placed on top of the trivet, or sometimes on top of the food, with the minimum liquid required underneath (refer to manufacturers' instructions).

Some models supply a pannier or raised basket which acts as a trivet and separator.

PRESSURE WEIGHT

This offers three pressures: High/15-lb., Medium/10-lb. and Low/5-lb.

There are two types of weight:

Weight A has a central plunger marked with three silver rings. The plunger rises and falls with the pressure inside the pressure cooker. One ring showing indicates Low/5-lb. pressure, two rings showing indicates Medium/10-lb. pressure, and three rings showing indicates High/15-lb. pressure. To position the weight, press it down on to the central vent until it clicks into place. Do not screw it on.

Weight B. The pressure is changed by unscrewing successive rings, three of which make up the complete weight. All three are used for High/15-lb. pressure, two are used for Medium/10-lb. pressure, and one is used for Low/5-lb. pressure. The small lifting ring on top of the weight should never be unscrewed. To position the weight, press it down on to the central vent and click it into position.

SPARE PARTS

Spare parts for your pressure cooker are usually available from your retailer. If not, contact the manufacturer direct. Quote the model number of your pressure cooker and the name and number of the part required. The address will be in the instruction book.

SOUPS AND STARTERS

Have you ever wished you had the time to make your own soup? Consider your wish granted. On the other hand, perhaps you *do* already prepare your own. Either way, your pressure cooker will save you hours of time and effort, since soups can be made in minutes. A good soup, we know, makes a delicious instant snack or starter, or a filling main meal.

Speedily prepared in the pressure cooker, some soups can be served later as a cold, light start to a meal. Or have you ever thought of making a cool fruit soup for a change? The family or your guests will appreciate the refreshing difference. Just cook the fruit in the pressure cooker with water, seasoning and a spice such as cinnamon. If you have a sweet tooth, a little sugar may be added. Chill and serve with a little white wine or cream stirred in.

The basis of most of my everyday soups is leftovers. For example, washed vegetable peelings and bones pressure-cooked with water, herbs and seasoning make an excellent stock – and one much more concentrated than those prepared in a saucepan. Portions of this concentrated stock can be used to flavour soups, main dishes, sauces or gravies. It is a good idea to keep a few cartons of home-made stock in the freezer.

SOUPS AND FREEZING

Most soups freeze well, so increase quantities, eating some and freezing the rest for another time. When cooking soup specifically for the freezer, it is a good idea to make it more concentrated so that it takes up less space. The extra liquid can be added on reheating.

To reheat frozen soup, pour the minimum amount of water recommended by the manufacturer into the pressure cooker (without the trivet) and add the block of soup. Bring to High/15-lb. pressure for 1–2 minutes, reducing pressure slowly, or 7½-lb. pressure for 2–4 minutes. You might need to add more thickening.

CHECKPOINTS FOR COOKING SOUPS

Do not fill the pressure cooker more than half-full with soup. The liquid must have room to boil up. If you wish to double or treble quantities (for freezing perhaps), cook the soup in batches (the time saved will still be worth it) or reduce the liquid in the recipe and add any extra when the soup has been cooked.

The trivet is not needed for stock and soup making.

Pressure-cooked soups require less seasoning since the ingredients retain more of their own mineral salts. Flavours are therefore more concentrated.

Thickening agents are best added after the main cooking.

Dried peas, beans, lentils etc. do not need overnight soaking for pressure cooking. Split pulses can be used as they are. Whole peas etc. are simply covered with boiling water and left for one hour before use.

When adapting your own favourite recipes for pressure cooking remember that there will be less evaporation, so the amount of liquid should be reduced (though always include the minimum amount recommended in the instruction book).

Where possible, pressure should be reduced slowly.

Stock

INGREDIENTS

	Imperial	Metric	American
Meat bones	2 lb.	1 kg	2 lb.
Water	2 pt	1.1 l.	5 cups
(If 7½-lb pressure)	3 pt	1.7 l.	7½ cups
Vegetables such as onions, carrots, celery, swede (or their washed peelings)			
Salt			
Black peppercorns			
Bay leaf			

Wash the bones and break them up as small as possible. Place the bones in the open pressure cooker with the water. Bring to the boil slowly, then skim the surface with a metal spoon or a draining spoon. Chop the vegetables and add them with the remaining ingredients, making sure that the cooker is not more than half full. Bring to pressure and cook for given time. Reduce pressure. Strain the stock and leave it to cool before removing surface fat.

COOKING TIME
High/15-lb. pressure 40 minutes
Reduce pressure slowly
Fixed 7½-lb. pressure 1 hour 20 minutes

TO FREEZE
Divide the stock into suitable quantities, pack and freeze it. Stock 'ice cubes' are useful for adding flavour to gravies etc.

Note: To make chicken stock, substitute a chicken carcass for the meat bones.

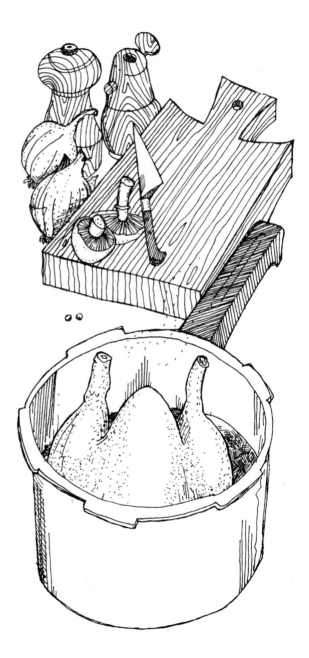

Thick Country Vegetable Soup

 Serves 6

INGREDIENTS	Imperial	Metric	American
Large onions	3	3	3
Large carrots	3	3	3
Large potatoes	3	3	3
Leek	1	1	1
Celery	4 sticks	4 sticks	4 stalks
Butter	1 oz.	25 g.	2 tbsp.
Cooking oil	1 tbsp.	1 tbsp.	1 tbsp.
Can tomatoes	8 oz.	226 g.	$\frac{1}{2}$ lb.
Chicken stock	$1\frac{1}{2}$ pt	1 l.	$3\frac{3}{4}$ cups
Bay leaves	2	2	2
Dried thyme	pinch	pinch	pinch
Salt and pepper			

Slice all vegetables about $\frac{1}{4}$ in./$\frac{1}{2}$ cm. thick. Heat the butter and oil in the open pressure cooker and in it sauté the vegetables gently for about 5 minutes. Add the tomatoes, including their juice, and all remaining ingredients. Stir well, bring to pressure and cook for given time. Reduce pressure. Discard bay leaves and serve.

COOKING TIME
High/15-lb. pressure 10 minutes
Reduce pressure slowly
Fixed $7\frac{1}{2}$-lb. pressure 20 minutes

TO FREEZE
Pack and freeze in the normal way.

Celery Soup

 Serves 4–6

INGREDIENTS	Imperial	Metric	American
Butter	1 oz.	25 g.	2 tbsp.
Large head celery, sliced	1	1	1
Onion, chopped	1	1	1
Water	$1\frac{3}{4}$ pt.	1 l.	4 cups
Salt and pepper			
Bouquet garni			
Milk	$\frac{1}{2}$ pt.	300 ml.	$1\frac{1}{4}$ cups

Heat the butter in the open pressure cooker and in it sauté the celery and onion gently for 2–3 minutes. Add the water, seasoning and bouquet garni. Bring to pressure and cook for given time. Reduce pressure. Remove the bouquet garni. Liquidize the soup and return it to the pressure cooker. Reheat it and stir in the milk just before serving.

COOKING TIME
High/15-lb. pressure 10 minutes
Reduce pressure slowly
Fixed $7\frac{1}{2}$-lb. pressure 20 minutes

TO FREEZE
Omit milk, pack and freeze. Stir in milk on reheating.

Lentil and Carrot Soup

 Serves 4

INGREDIENTS

	Imperial	Metric	American
Butter	1 oz.	25 g.	2 tbsp.
Rashers streaky bacon or slices bacon, chopped	4	4	4
Onion, chopped	1	1	1
Carrots, diced	8 oz.	225 g.	½ lb.
Lentils	4 oz.	100 g.	¼ lb.
Salt and pepper			
Bouquet garni			
Chicken stock	1½ pt.	900 ml.	3¾ cups

Heat the butter in the open pressure cooker and in it sauté the bacon, onion and carrots gently for 4–5 minutes. Stir in the remaining ingredients, bring to pressure and cook for given time. Reduce pressure.

Remove bouquet garni and adjust seasoning if necessary. If a smoother consistency is preferred, liquidize or sieve the soup.

COOKING TIME

High/15-lb. pressure 10 minutes
Reduce pressure slowly
Fixed 7½-lb. pressure 20 minutes

TO FREEZE

Omit bouquet garni, pack and freeze. On reheating add a pinch of mixed herbs.

Cream of Cauliflower Soup

 Serves 4

INGREDIENTS

	Imperial	Metric	American
Medium cauliflower, chopped	1	1	1
Chicken stock	1½ pt	900 ml.	4 cups
Butter	1 oz.	25 g.	2 tbsp.
Salt and pepper			
Pinch ground nutmeg			
Single or thin cream	¼ pt	150 ml.	⅔ cup

Place all the ingredients, except the cream into the pressure cooker. Bring to pressure and cook for given time. Reduce pressure. Liquidize the soup and return it to the pressure cooker. Reheat and stir in the cream just before serving.

COOKING TIME

High/15-lb. pressure 4 minutes
Reduce pressure slowly
Fixed 7½-lb. pressure 8 minutes

TO FREEZE

Omit cream, pack and freeze. Stir in cream on reheating, just before serving.

CHECKPOINT

Do not boil the soup after adding the cream.

French Onion Soup

 Serves 4

INGREDIENTS

	Imperial	Metric	American
Butter	1 oz.	25 g.	2 tbsp.
Onions, sliced	1 lb.	450 g.	1 lb.
Beef stock	2 pt	1.1 l.	5 cups
Salt and pepper			
Bay leaf			
Slices of french bread			
Grated Gruyère or			
Cheddar cheese			

Heat the butter in the open pressure cooker and gently sauté the onions in it until golden brown. Stir in the stock, season well and add bay leaf. Bring to pressure and cook for given time. Reduce pressure. Remove bay leaf. Ladle the soup into an ovenproof bowl. Float the slices of French bread on top of the soup and top them with grated cheese. Place the bowl under a hot grill for 2–3 minutes until the cheese bubbles. Serve immediately.

COOKING TIME

High/15-lb. pressure 4 minutes
Reduce pressure slowly
Fixed 7½-lb. pressure 8 minutes

TO FREEZE

Pack and freeze the soup without bread and cheese.

Tomato Soup

 Serves 4–6

INGREDIENTS

	Imperial	Metric	American
Butter	1 oz.	25 g.	2 tbsp.
Celery, chopped	1 stick	1 stick	1 stalk
Carrot, chopped	1	1	1
Onion, chopped	1	1	1
Rashers streaky bacon, chopped	3	3	3
Tomatoes, skinned and sliced	1½ lb.	700 g.	1½ lb.
Beef stock	1 pt	550 ml.	2½ cups
Pinch mixed herbs			
Pinch sugar			
Salt and pepper, chopped parsley			

Heat the butter in the open pressure cooker and gently sauté the celery, carrot, onion and bacon in it for 2–3 minutes. Add remaining ingredients, except parsley, bring to pressure and cook for given time. Reduce pressure. Serve garnished with chopped parsley.

COOKING TIME

High/15-lb. pressure 4 minutes
Reduce pressure slowly
Fixed 7½-lb. pressure 8 minutes

TO FREEZE

Pack and freeze in the normal way. Garnish at reheating stage.

Note: This soup can be made with canned tomatoes. To make Cream of Tomato Soup, liquidize or sieve the cooked soup and stir in ¼ pt/150 ml./⅔ cup cream before serving.

If the finished soup lacks colour, stir in a little tomato purée or ketchup.

Cream of Mushroom Soup

Serves 4–6

INGREDIENTS	Imperial	Metric	American
Butter	2 oz.	50 g.	¼ cup
Mushrooms, sliced	8 oz.	225 g.	½ lb.
Chicken stock	1 pt	550 ml.	2½ cups
Salt and pepper			
Flour	2 tbsp.	2 tbsp.	2 tbsp.
Milk	¾ pt	400 ml.	2 cups
Chopped parsley	2 tbsp.	2 tbsp.	2 tbsp.

Melt the butter in the open pressure cooker and gently sauté the mushrooms in it for a few minutes. Add the stock and season well. Bring to pressure and cook for given time. Reduce pressure. Mix the flour with a little cold water to form a smooth paste and add this to the soup. Bring to the boil. Stir in the milk and parsley before serving.

COOKING TIME

High/15-lb. pressure 5 minutes
Reduce pressure slowly
Fixed 7½-lb. pressure 10 minutes

TO FREEZE

Omit milk and parsley, pack and freeze. Stir in milk and parsley on reheating.

Potage Darblay

Serves 6

INGREDIENTS	Imperial	Metric	American
Butter	2 oz.	50 g.	¼ cup
Potatoes, thinly sliced	1 lb.	450 g.	1 lb.
Onion, thinly sliced	1	1	1
Water	¾ pt	400 ml.	2 cups
Bay leaf			
Salt and pepper			
Milk	¾ pt	400 ml.	2 cups
To garnish:			
Carrot, cut in thin strips	1	1	1
Celery, cut in thin strips	1 stick	1 stick	1 stalk
Onion, thinly sliced	1	1	1

Heat the butter in the open pressure cooker and gently sauté the potatoes and onion in it for 2–3 minutes. Add the water and bay leaf and season well.

Arrange the vegetables to be used as garnish in a separator and sit this on top of the soup. Bring to pressure and cook for given time. Reduce pressure.

Remove separator containing the vegetables and set it to one side. Discard bay leaf. Liquidize the soup and return it to the pressure cooker. Stir in the milk, check the seasoning and reheat. Garnish with the cooked vegetables and serve.

COOKING TIME

High/15-lb. pressure 8 minutes
Reduce pressure slowly
Fixed 7½-lb. pressure 15 minutes

TO FREEZE

Omit milk, pack and freeze. Freeze vegetables separately. Stir in milk on reheating and garnish with the vegetables.

Oxtail Soup

Serves 4–6

INGREDIENTS	Imperial	Metric	American
Cooking oil	1 tbsp.	1 tbsp.	1 tbsp.
Oxtail, jointed	1	1	1
Onions, chopped	2	2	2
Celery, sliced	2 sticks	2 sticks	2 stalks
Carrot, sliced	1	1	1
Beef stock	2 pt	1.1 l.	5 cups
(If 7½-lb pressure)	3 pt	1.7 l.	7½ cups
Bouquet garni			
Salt and pepper			
Butter	1 oz.	25 g.	2 tbsp.
Flour	2–3 tbsp.	2–3 tbsp.	2–3 tbsp.
Lemon juice	1 tsp.	1 tsp.	1 tsp.

Heat the cooking oil in the open pressure cooker and in it sauté the oxtail and the vegetables gently for 4–5 minutes. Add the stock and bouquet garni and season well. Bring to pressure and cook for given time. Reduce pressure. Strain the soup. Remove meat from the bones and cut it into small pieces.

Cool the stock (preferably overnight), then skim off the surface fat. In the open pressure cooker or a saucepan, melt the butter. Add the flour and cook gently for a few minutes, stirring well. Slowly add the oxtail stock and bring to the boil, stirring continuously. Add the meat pieces. Adjust seasoning if necessary and add lemon juice just before serving.

COOKING TIME
High/15-lb. pressure 40 minutes
Reduce pressure slowly
Fixed 7½-lb. pressure 1 hour 15 minutes

TO FREEZE
Omit lemon, pack and freeze.

Minestrone

 Serves 4–6

INGREDIENTS

	Imperial	Metric	American
Butter	1 oz.	25 g.	2 tbsp.
Rashers streaky bacon, or slices bacon, chopped	3	3	3
Onion, chopped	1	1	1
Clove garlic, crushed	1	1	1
Leek, sliced	1	1	1
Carrot	1	1	1
Celery, sliced	1 stick	1 stick	1 stalk
Cabbage, shredded	$\frac{1}{4}$	$\frac{1}{4}$	$\frac{1}{4}$
Runner beans or green beans, sliced	4	4	4
Peas, shelled	1 oz.	25 g.	$\frac{1}{4}$ cup
Tomato purée/paste	2 tbsp.	2 tbsp.	2 tbsp.
Salt and pepper			
Chicken stock or water	2 pt	1.1 l.	5 cups
Macaroni, spaghetti or pasta shapes	1 oz.	25 g.	$\frac{1}{4}$ cup

Heat the butter in the open pressure cooker and in it sauté the bacon and vegetables gently for 2–3 minutes. Add the remaining ingredients, bring to pressure and cook for given time. Reduce pressure. Adjust seasoning if necessary.

COOKING TIME

High/15-lb. pressure 8 minutes
Reduce pressure slowly
Fixed 7½-lb. pressure 15 minutes

TO FREEZE

Omit garlic, pack and freeze. Add garlic at reheating stage and simmer for 5 minutes. Alternatively, season with garlic salt.

Note: Vegetables for this soup may be varied according to the season.

Potato and Mint Soup

 Serves 4

INGREDIENTS

	Imperial	Metric	American
Butter	1 oz.	25 g.	2 tbsp.
Potatoes, sliced	1 lb.	450 g.	1 lb.
Water	1½ pt	900 ml.	3¾ cups
Salt and pepper			
Sprigs mint	3–4	3–4	3–4
Milk	½ pt	300 ml.	1¼ cups

Heat the butter in the open pressure cooker and in it sauté the potatoes gently for 2–3 minutes. Stir in the water and season well. Add mint, bring to pressure and cook for given time. Reduce pressure. Liquidize or sieve the soup, then return it to the pressure cooker. Stir in milk, reheat and serve. Garnish with a few sprigs of mint.

COOKING TIME

High/15-lb. pressure 5 minutes
Reduce pressure slowly
Fixed 7½-lb. pressure 10 minutes

TO FREEZE

Omit milk, pack and freeze. Stir in milk on reheating.

Cock-a-Leekie

 Serves 4–6

INGREDIENTS

	Imperial	Metric	American
Chicken joints	3	3	3
Leeks, chopped	1 lb.	450 g.	1 lb.
Chicken stock	1½ pt	1 l.	3¾ cups
Salt			
Black pepper			

Place the chicken joints and leeks in the pressure cooker and pour in the stock. Season well. Bring to pressure and cook for given time. Reduce pressure.

Remove the chicken joints from the pressure cooker and, when cooled sufficiently, remove the meat from the bones, breaking it into pieces. Return the chicken pieces to the pressure cooker. Adjust seasoning, if necessary, reheat and serve.

COOKING TIME

High/15-lb. pressure 7 minutes
Reduce pressure slowly
Fixed 7½-lb. pressure 12 minutes

TO FREEZE

Pack and freeze in the normal way.

Thick Pea Soup

 Serves 4–6

INGREDIENTS

	Imperial	Metric	American
Dried peas	6 oz.	175 g.	1½ cups
Butter	1 oz.	25 g.	2 tbsp.
Medium onion, chopped	1	1	1
Rashers streaky bacon or slices bacon, chopped	6	6	6
Chicken stock			
Pinch dried marjoram			
Salt and pepper			
Milk	¼ pt.	150 ml.	⅔ cup

Place the peas in a bowl and cover them with boiling water. Cover with a plate and leave to stand for 1 hour. Heat the butter in the open pressure cooker and in it sauté the onion and bacon gently for a few minutes. Strain the peas, reserving the liquid, and add these to the onion mixture. Make up the soaking liquid from the peas to 1½ pt/900 ml./3¾ cups, using chicken stock. Add the stock and marjoram to the pressure cooker, then season well. Bring to pressure and cook for given time. Reduce pressure. Liquidize the soup and just before serving stir in the milk.

COOKING TIME

High/15-lb. pressure 20 minutes
Reduce pressure slowly
Fixed 7½-lb. pressure 40 minutes

TO FREEZE

Omit milk, pack and freeze. Stir in milk on reheating (a little extra might be needed after freezing).

Savoury Starters

 Serves 4

INGREDIENTS

	Imperial	Metric	American
Butter	1 tbsp.	1 tbsp.	1 tbsp.
Small onion, chopped	1	1	1
Tomato, skinned and chopped	1	1	1
Made mustard	1 tsp.	1 tsp.	1 tsp.
Salt and pepper			
Eggs	4	4	4
Milk	4 tbsp.	4 tbsp.	4 tbsp.
Mushrooms, chopped	4	4	4
Toasted breadcrumbs			

Butter four individual ovenproof dishes. Mix together the onion, tomato and mustard, seasoning well with salt and pepper. Divide the mixture among the four dishes. Beat together the eggs, milk and mushrooms. Season and pour into each dish. Cap the dishes with foil, making sure the caps are tightly secured. Pour ½ pt/300 ml./1¼ cups water into the pressure cooker, position the trivet and sit the dishes on it. Bring to pressure and cook for given time. Reduce pressure.

Sprinkle with toasted breadcrumbs and serve immediately.

COOKING TIME
High/15-lb. pressure 3 minutes
Reduce pressure slowly
Fixed 7½-lb. pressure 6 minutes

CHECKPOINT
Make sure the dishes do not touch the sides of the pressure cooker; they could crack. If necessary, stand three in a triangle with the fourth centred on top. Alternatively, cook them in two batches – it takes only a few minutes extra.

Farmhouse Paté

 Serves 8–10

INGREDIENTS

	Imperial	Metric	American
Streaky bacon, de-rinded	4 oz.	100 g.	¼ lb.
Butter	2 oz.	50 g.	¼ cup
Lambs' liver, chopped	1 lb.	450 g.	1 lb.
Chickens' livers, chopped	8 oz.	225 g.	½ lb.
Small onion, chopped	1	1	1
Clove garlic, crushed	1	1	1
Salt, black pepper			
Milk	½ pt	300 ml.	1¼ cups
Flour	1½ oz.	40 g.	⅓ cup
Thyme	½ tsp.	½ tsp.	½ tsp.

Stretch the bacon with the blade of a knife, then use it to line a suitable ovenproof container (to fit easily into pressure cooker). In a frying pan heat the butter and in it lightly brown the livers, onion and garlic. Season well with salt and black pepper. Liquidize the liver mixture together with all remaining ingredients. Pour into the prepared container and fold the ends of the bacon on to the pâté. Cover securely with foil. Pour 1 pt/550 ml./2½ cups water into the pressure cooker, position the trivet and sit the pâté on top. Bring to pressure and cook for given time. Reduce pressure. Place a saucer/plate/stiff piece of cardboard on the pâté (this should fit neatly inside the container) with a weight on top and allow it to cool before turning it out.

COOKING TIME
High/15-lb. pressure 25 minutes
Reduce pressure slowly
Fixed 7½-lb. pressure 45 minutes

TO FREEZE
For convenience, freeze the pâté in slices, interleaved with polythene film and pack in foil.

MEAT

The pressure cooker cooks meat beautifully, particularly the tougher cuts which are usually less expensive than the best but have just as much flavour and nutritional value. The time saving is enormous, while the result is tender and moist.

Pot-roast joints make a nourishing meal with the vegetables cooked alongside. Make the stock into a tasty gravy to accompany the meat and vegetables. Try cooking a bacon joint in your pressure cooker – there's then no need to soak it overnight (see page 28).

I think casseroles are my favourite pressure-cooked meals. The concentrated flavour makes them something special. Try your own favourite casserole in the pressure cooker.

MEAT AND FREEZING

Most meat dishes cooked in the pressure cooker can be frozen. Specific instructions are given in the recipes where freezing is recommended.

Joints can be pressure-cooked when still frozen; beef is particularly good cooked this way. Allow 10 minutes extra per 1 lb./450 g. at High/15-lb. pressure, or 20 minutes extra at fixed 7½-lb. pressure.

Frozen stewing steak etc. need not be thawed before pressure-cooking. Partially-frozen meat is easier to handle anyway. Add 5 minutes to the cooking time for High/15-lb. pressure or 10 minutes for fixed 7½ lb. pressure.

Minced meat should always be thawed before cooking; otherwise it tends to stick together in clumps.

Suet puddings should be frozen with the pastry uncooked – so that it is not cooked twice. Thaw them out thoroughly before pressure-cooking.

Cooked meat dishes can also be reheated in your pressure cooker from the frozen state. Just pour the minimum amount of liquid recommended by the manufacturer into the pressure cooker and add the block of frozen food (use the trivet if the prepared dish is in a covered foil container, for example). Bring to pressure and cook for 10–12 minutes at High/15-lb. pressure or 20–25 minutes at fixed 7½-lb. pressure. The size, shape and content of the frozen block of food will obviously cause these times to vary slightly. Extra thickening may be necessary after reheating. To reheat individual portions, place the block of food in an unperforated separator with the trivet and the minimum amount of liquid beneath it. Bring to pressure as before. Pressure can be reduced with cold water where suitable.

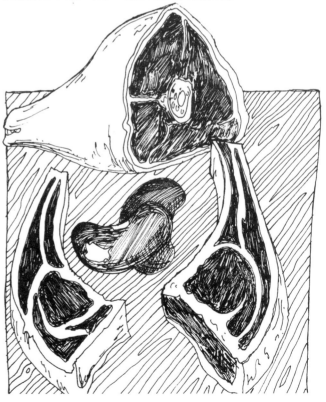

CHECKPOINTS FOR MEATS

Do not fill the pressure cooker more than half full with casserole-type dishes. The liquid must have space to boil up.

Use the trivet for pot-roasting joints of meat and for steaming suet puddings (where the food is to be cooked in the steam). Casseroles and stews do not require the use of the trivet.

The cooking time for a joint depends on its size and shape, and on the amount of bone and fat present. You will soon get used to timing cooking so that the meat is done to your liking. The joint can easily be brought to pressure for an extra few minutes if not quite cooked. The table opposite gives cooking times per 1 lb./450 g. meat. Joints up to 3 lb./1.5 kg. can be prepared in the pressure cooker. Above this weight, cooking may be uneven through the joint. Remember too that the joint must fit into the pressure cooker with enough space to allow steam to circulate. You may also wish to leave room for vegetables.

Remember to use the minimum amount of liquid (stock, water, wine, cider etc.) recommended by the manufacturer. When cooking joints, the amount of liquid needed will depend on the cooking time. Your instruction book will suggest the correct amount for your particular model.

Thickening agents are best added after cooking, though in a few recipes I have suggested coating the raw meat with seasoned flour.

To serve vegetables with a joint or with braised meat, reduce pressure a few minutes before the end of cooking time, add the vegetables and bring to pressure again for the required time.

Meat cooked in a pressure cooker is usually browned in hot butter, oil, lard or dripping first. Since there is no browning action in the pressure cooker, this improves the appearance, particularly of joints, as well as the flavour of the finished dish.

Use less seasoning than you would usually.

When adapting your own recipes for pressure-cooking, less liquid will probably be needed since pressure-cooking means less evaporation.

The following times for pressure-cooking joints are for High/15-lb. pressure. If your pressure cooker is fixed at 7½-lb., just double the time per pound and follow the manufacturers' instructions on the amount of liquid to use.

	Cooking time per lb./450 g. at High/ 15 lb. pressure
Beef	
Rolled sirloin or rump	10 minutes
Topside, rolled rump	12 minutes
Silverside	15 minutes
Lamb	
Breast, boned and rolled	12 minutes
Leg	15 minutes
Pork	
Fillet	12 minutes
Shoulder or loin, boned & rolled	15 minutes
Veal	
Knuckle	10 minutes
Fillet, loin	12 minutes
Shoulder, boned or breast, boned and rolled	14 minutes
Bacon	12 minutes
Ox tongue	15 minutes

Sherry Bacon

 Serves 4–6

INGREDIENTS	Imperial	Metric	American
Bacon joint	2¼ lb.	1.1 kg.	2¼ lb.
Butter	1 oz.	25 g.	2 tbsp.
Large onion, sliced	1	1	1
Large carrot, sliced	1	1	1
Celery, sliced	1 stick	1 stick	1 stalk
Sherry	4 tbsp.	4 tbsp.	4 tbsp.
Tomato purée/ paste	1 tbsp.	1 tbsp.	1 tbsp.
Water	¾ pt	400 ml.	2 cups
(If 7½-lb. pressure)	1 pt	550 ml.	2½ cups
Bouquet garni			
Black peppercorns	6	6	6
Flour	3 tbsp.	3 tbsp.	3 tbsp.

Place the bacon joint in the pressure cooker,
cover it with cold water and bring slowly to the boil.
Discard the water and dry the bacon with kitchen
paper. Heat the butter in the open pressure cooker
and brown the bacon joint on all sides. Remove from
the pressure cooker. Place into the pressure cooker
all remaining ingredients, except flour, and mix well.
Place trivet on top of the vegetable mixture and
position bacon joint on the trivet. Bring to pressure
and cook for given time. Reduce pressure. Slice the
bacon, arrange it on a serving dish and keep it warm.
Strain the sauce and return the liquid to the open
pressure cooker. Mix the flour with a little cold water
to form a smooth paste and stir it into the sauce.
Bring to the boil, stirring well. Pour a little over the
bacon and serve the rest separately.

COOKING TIME
High/15-lb. pressure 30 minutes
Reduce pressure slowly
Fixed 7½-lb. pressure 1 hour

TO FREEZE
Pack left over slices of bacon with sauce poured
over in a foil tray. Cover and freeze.

Pineapple Bacon

 Serves 4

INGREDIENTS

	Imperial	Metric	American
Unsmoked bacon collar or slipper joint, cut into cubes	1½ lb.	700 g.	1½ lb.
Butter	1 oz.	25 g.	2 tbsp.
Onions, chopped	2	2	2
Canned pineapple chunks	15½-oz.	439-g.	1 lb.
Chicken stock			
Dried red chillies	2	2	2
Paprika pepper	1 tsp.	1 tsp.	1 tsp.
Bay leaves	2	2	2
Flour	2 tbsp.	2 tbsp.	2 tbsp.

Place the bacon cubes in the open pressure cooker and cover with cold water. Bring slowly to the boil. Discard the liquid and dry the bacon cubes with kitchen paper. Heat the butter in the open pressure cooker and in it sauté the onions and bacon gently for 3–4 minutes. Make up the juice from the pineapple to ½ pt/300 ml./1¼ cups with chicken stock (¾ pt/400 ml./2 cups if fixed 7½-lb. pressure) and stir it into the bacon mixture. Add the chillies, paprika pepper and bay leaves. Bring to pressure and cook for given time. Reduce pressure.

Remove chillies and bay leaves. Mix the flour with a little cold water to form a smooth paste and stir this into the bacon. Bring to the boil, stirring continuously. Add the pineapple chunks, reheat and serve.

COOKING TIME
High/15-lb. pressure 20 minutes
Reduce pressure slowly
Fixed 7½-lb. pressure 35 minutes

Bacon Casserole with Dumplings

 Serves 4

INGREDIENTS

	Imperial	Metric	American
Bacon collar or slipper joint, cut into cubes	1½ lb.	700 g.	1½ lb.
Butter	1 oz.	25 g.	2 tbsp.
Leeks, sliced	1 lb.	450 g.	1 lb.
Chicken stock	¾ pt	400 ml.	2 cups
Black pepper			
Dumplings:			
Self-raising flour or flour sifted with 1 tsp. baking powder	4 oz.	100 g.	1 cup
Shredded or finely-chopped suet	2 oz.	50 g.	½ cup
Small onion, finely chopped	1	1	1
Salt and pepper			
Pinch herbs, such as sage or thyme			
Cold water	4 tbsp.	4 tbsp.	4 tbsp.

Place the bacon cubes in the open pressure cooker and cover them with cold water. Bring slowly to the boil. Discard the liquid and dry the bacon cubes with kitchen paper.

Heat the butter in the open pressure cooker and in it sauté the leeks and bacon lightly for 3–4 minutes. Add the chicken stock and black pepper. Bring to pressure and cook for given time. Reduce pressure.

Mix together the ingredients for the dumplings, forming the soft dough into eight balls.

Return the open pressure cooker to the heat, bring to the boil and add the dumplings. Place the lid on the pressure cooker *without the weight or valve* and simmer for 10–15 minutes.

COOKING TIME
High/15-lb. pressure 20 minutes
Reduce pressure slowly
Fixed 7½-lb. pressure 35 minutes

TO FREEZE
Pack meat mixture into rigid polythene container, cover and freeze. The dumplings are best prepared at the reheating stage.

Note: If a thicker casserole is preferred, stir in some flour mixed to a smooth paste with cold water before adding the dumplings.

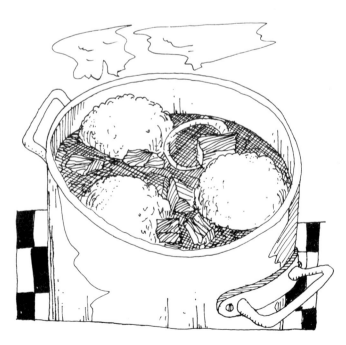

Bacon in Red Wine

 Serves 4

INGREDIENTS

	Imperial	Metric	American
Bacon joint, such as forehock, cut into cubes	1½ lb.	700 g.	1½ lb.
Butter	1 oz.	25 g.	2 tbsp.
Button mushrooms	4 oz.	100 g.	¼ lb.
Celery, sliced	2 sticks	2 sticks	2 stalks
Grated rind and juice 1 orange			
Red wine	½ pt	300 ml.	1¼ cups
(If 7½-lb. pressure) pressure)	¾ pt	400 ml.	2 cups
Ground black pepper			
Cornflour/cornstarch	2 tbsp.	2 tbsp.	2 tbsp.

Place the bacon pieces in the open pressure cooker. Cover with cold water and bring to the boil slowly. Discard the water and dry the bacon pieces on kitchen paper. Heat the butter in the open pressure cooker and brown the bacon lightly. Stir in the remaining ingredients (except cornflour). Bring to pressure and cook for given time. Reduce pressure. Mix the cornflour with a little cold water to form a smooth paste; stir it into the bacon mixture. Bring to the boil, stirring continuously. Delicious with rice or green salad.

COOKING TIME
High/15-lb. pressure 20 minutes
Reduce pressure with cold water
Fixed 7½-lb. pressure 35 minutes

Chilli Kidneys

 ❄ Serves 4

INGREDIENTS

	Imperial	Metric	American
Lambs'/sheep's kidneys	12	12	12
Butter	1 oz.	25 g.	2 tbsp.
Medium onions, chopped	2	2	2
Tabasco sauce	1 tsp.	1 tsp.	1 tsp.
Chilli sauce	2 tsp.	2 tsp.	2 tsp.
Worcestershire sauce	2 tsp.	2 tsp.	2 tsp.
Made mustard	2 tsp.	2 tsp.	2 tsp.
Tomato purée/paste	2 tbsp.	2 tbsp.	2 tbsp.
Beef stock	½ pt	300 ml.	1¼ cups

Skin, core and slice the kidneys. Heat the butter in the open pressure cooker and in it sauté the onions lightly till transparent. Add the kidneys and brown them lightly to seal in the juices. Add remaining ingredients, stirring well. Bring to pressure and cook for given time. Reduce pressure.

COOKING TIME
High 15-lb. pressure 5 minutes
Reduce pressure with cold water
Fixed 7½-lb. pressure 10 minutes

TO FREEZE
Pack in rigid polythene container, cover and freeze.

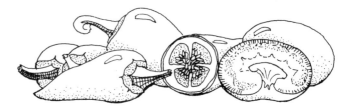

Beef in Brown Ale with Cheesy Topping

Serves 4

INGREDIENTS

	Imperial	Metric	American
Lard	2 oz.	50 g.	$\frac{1}{4}$ cup
Chuck steak, cut into cubes	$1\frac{1}{4}$ lb.	600 g.	$1\frac{1}{4}$ lb.
Onions, sliced	8 oz.	225 g.	$\frac{1}{2}$ lb.
Mushrooms, sliced	4 oz.	100 g.	$\frac{1}{4}$ lb.
Brown ale	$\frac{1}{2}$ pt	300 ml.	$1\frac{1}{4}$ cups
(If $7\frac{1}{2}$-lb. pressure)	$\frac{3}{4}$ pt	400 ml.	2 cups
Beef stock	$\frac{1}{4}$ pt	150 ml.	$\frac{2}{3}$ cup
Made mustard	1 tsp.	1 tsp.	1 tsp.
Sugar	2 tsp.	2 tsp.	2 tsp.
Salt and black pepper			
Flour	2 tbsp.	2 tbsp.	2 tbsp.
Topping:			
Small French loaf	1	1	1
Butter	3 oz.	75 g.	6 tbsp.
Cheese, finely grated	4 oz.	100 g.	$\frac{1}{4}$ lb.

Heat the lard in the open pressure cooker and brown the meat lightly. Lift it out with a draining spoon. In the same lard, sauté the onions and mushrooms for 2–3 minutes. Replace meat. Add brown ale, beef stock, mustard and sugar, and season well with salt and black pepper. Bring to pressure and cook for given time. Reduce pressure.

Mix the flour with a little cold water to form a smooth paste and stir it into beef mixture. Bring to the boil, stirring well. Arrange meat mixture in an ovenproof serving dish.

Cut the bread into thick slices and spread one side of each slice with mustard. Cream the butter, beat in the cheese and season to taste. Spread cheese mixture thickly on opposite side of each slice of bread. Then place bread, cheese side upwards, on top of the beef. Brown under hot grill till topping is crisp and golden.

COOKING TIME

High/15-lb. pressure 20 minutes
Reduce pressure slowly
Fixed $7\frac{1}{2}$-lb. pressure 40 minutes

TO FREEZE

Omit bread and cheese topping. Pack into rigid polythene container, cover and freeze.

Steak and Kidney Pudding

Serves 4

INGREDIENTS	Imperial	Metric	American
Filling:			
Stewing steak, cut into cubes	12 oz.	350 g.	¾ lb.
Sheep kidneys, skinned and chopped	4 oz.	100 g.	¼ lb.
Seasoned flour			
Onion, chopped	1	1	1
Salt and pepper			
Beef stock	½ pt.	300 ml.	1¼ cups
(If 7½-lb. pressure)	¾ pt	400 ml.	2 cups
Suet pastry:			
Self-raising flour, or flour sifted with 2 tsp. baking powder	8 oz.	225 g.	2 cups
Pinch salt			
Shredded suet	4 oz.	100 g.	¾–1 cup
Cold water	¼ pt	150 ml.	⅔ cup

Coat the steak and the kidney pieces with seasoned flour. Into the open pressure cooker place the meat, onion, seasoning and beef stock. Bring to pressure and cook for given time. Reduce pressure.

Meanwhile, sieve together the flour and salt and stir in the suet. Mix with the cold water to form an elastic dough. Roll two-thirds of the dough into a circle and use it to line a greased 1½-pt/1 l. basin. Put the steak and kidney in the middle with half of the gravy. Dampen the edges of the dough. Roll remaining dough into a circle and use it to cover the pudding. Press edges together firmly and trim. Cover securely with a piece of foil (make a pleat in the foil to allow the pudding to rise). Pour in 2½ pt/1·5 l./6½ cups water into pressure cooker,

position the trivet and stand the pudding on top. Close the pressure cooker (do not position the weight) and place it on the heat. When steam begins to escape from the vent in the lid, lower the heat and steam it gently (without the weight) for 15 minutes. Increase the heat, bring to pressure and cook for given time. Reduce pressure.

Serve the pudding from the basin. Heat remaining gravy and serve separately.

COOKING TIME
Meat mixture:
High/15-lb. pressure 15 minutes
Reduce pressure slowly
Fixed 7½-lb. pressure 30 minutes

Pudding:
Pre-steaming 15 minutes
Low/5-lb. pressure 25 minutes
Reduce pressure slowly
Fixed 7½-lb. pressure 40 minutes

Note: Pre-steaming is important since this helps give a light result to the suet pastry.

Pepperpot Beef

 Serves 4

INGREDIENTS	Imperial	Metric	American
Brisket of beef, rolled	2½ lb.	1.1 kg.	2½ lb.
Freshly-ground black pepper	1 tbsp.	1 tbsp.	1 tbsp.
Cooking oil	2 tbsp.	2 tbsp.	2 tbsp.
Large onion, sliced	1	1	1
Leek, sliced	1	1	1
Carrots, sliced	4	4	4
Salt			
Beef stock	¾ pt	400 ml.	2 cups
(If 7½-lb. pressure)	1 pt	550 ml.	2½ cups
Bay leaves	2	2	2
Flour	2–3 tbsp.	2–3 tbsp.	2–3 tbsp.

Press the ground pepper well into all sides of the beef. Heat the oil in open pressure cooker and in it brown the beef quickly on all sides. Remove meat and in the same oil, sauté the vegetables till lightly browned, seasoning with salt. Lift out. Add the stock and bay leaves to any remaining oil and position the trivet. Place beef on it. Bring to pressure and cook for given time. Reduce pressure.

Place the vegetables around the beef and bring to pressure again for given time. Reduce pressure. Arrange them on a dish and keep warm. Remove bay leaves. Mix the flour with a little cold water to form a smooth paste and stir it into the stock. Bring to the boil, stirring continuously. Serve separately.

COOKING TIME
High/15-lb. pressure beef 25 minutes
Reduce pressure with cold water
    vegetables added 5 minutes
Reduce pressure slowly
Fixed 7½-lb. pressure beef 50 minutes
    vegetables added 10 minutes

Beef Goulash

 Serves 4

INGREDIENTS

	Imperial	Metric	American
Stewing steak, cut into cubes	1½ lb.	700 g.	1½ lb.
Seasoned flour			
Butter	2 oz.	50 g.	¼ cup
Large onion, chopped	1	1	1
Paprika pepper	3 tsp.	3 tsp.	3 tsp.
Tomato purée/paste	2 tbsp.	2 tbsp.	2 tbsp.
Beef stock	¾ pt	400 ml.	2 cups
(If 7½-lb. pressure)	1 pt	550 ml.	2½ cups
Salt and pepper			
Carton soured cream/ natural unsweetened yoghurt	6 fl.-oz.	175 ml.	⅔ cup
Chopped parsley			

Coat the stewing steak with seasoned flour. Heat
the butter in the open pressure cooker and brown
the meat on all sides. Add the onion and cook for
a further 1–2 minutes, then stir in the paprika
pepper, tomato purée and beef stock. Season well.
Bring to pressure and cook for given time. Reduce
pressure. Stir in soured cream just before serving and
garnish with chopped parsley. Serve with buttered
noodles.

COOKING TIME
High/15-lb. pressure 20 minutes
Reduce pressure slowly
Fixed 7½-lb. pressure 40 minutes

TO FREEZE
Omit soured cream. Pack into rigid polythene
container, cover and freeze. Add soured cream on
reheating.

Thrifty Beef Roll

Serves 6

INGREDIENTS

	Imperial	Metric	American
Minced beef/ hamburger	1 lb.	450 g.	1 lb.
Medium onion, finely chopped	1	1	1
Breadcrumbs	3 oz.	75 g.	1½ cups
Salt	2 tsp.	2 tsp.	2 tsp.
Black pepper	1 tsp.	1 tsp.	1 tsp.
Tomato purée/paste	3 tbsp.	3 tbsp.	3 tbsp.
Mixed herbs	1 tsp.	1 tsp.	1 tsp.
Filling:			
Cheddar cheese, finely grated	4 oz.	100 g.	¼ lb.
Chopped parsley	1 tbsp.	1 tbsp.	1 tbsp.
Made mustard	1 tbsp.	1 tbsp.	1 tbsp.
Garnish:			
Little grated cheese			

Mix together the minced beef, onion, breadcrumbs, salt, pepper, tomato purée and mixed herbs. Spread the mixture thickly on a sheet of greaseproof paper (the mixture should measure about 7 in./18 cm. × 10 in./25 cm.). Mix together the ingredients for the filling and spread it carefully over the meat. Using the greaseproof paper as an aid, roll up the beef and shape it firmly. Butter a piece of foil and place the beef roll on this.

Pour ½ pt/300 ml./1¼ cups water into pressure cooker (1 pt/550 ml./2½ cups if fixed 7½-lb. pressure), position the trivet and sit the beef roll on top. Bring to pressure and cook for given time. Reduce pressure.

Carefully lift out the beef roll and place it on a serving dish. Sprinkle a little grated cheese along the length of the roll and brown it under a hot grill before serving.

COOKING TIME
High/15-lb. pressure 20 minutes
Reduce pressure slowly
Fixed 7½-lb. pressure 40 minutes

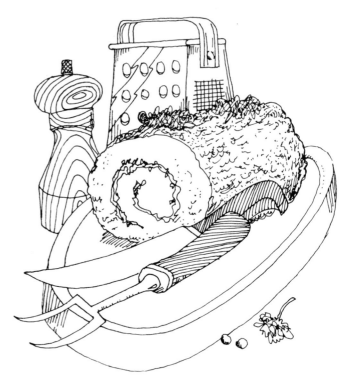

Beef Pot Roast

 Serves 4–6

INGREDIENTS

	Imperial	Metric	American
Beef topside	*2 lb.*	*1 kg.*	*2 lb.*
Salt and pepper			
Butter	*1 oz.*	*25 g.*	*2 tbsp.*
Cooking oil	*1 tbsp.*	*1 tbsp.*	*1 tbsp.*
Onion, chopped	*1*	*1*	*1*
Potatoes, halved	*4–6*	*4–6*	*4–6*
Carrots, sliced	*4*	*4*	*4*
Celery, cut up	*4 sticks*	*4 sticks*	*4 stalks*
Beef stock	*$\frac{3}{4}$ pt*	*400 ml.*	*2 cups*
(If 7$\frac{1}{2}$-lb. pressure)	*1 pt*	*550 ml.*	*2$\frac{1}{2}$ cups*
Cornflour or cornstarch	*2 tbsp.*	*2 tbsp.*	*2 tbsp.*

Season the topside well with salt and pepper. Heat the butter and oil in the open pressure cooker and brown the beef on all sides. Lift out. In the same fat, sauté the vegetables gently for 2–3 minutes, seasoning well. Lift out with a draining spoon. Pour the stock on to any remaining fat in the pressure cooker, position the trivet and sit the beef on top. Bring to pressure and cook for given time. Reduce pressure. Put the vegetables around the beef, bring to pressure again and cook for given time. Reduce pressure. Arrange on a dish and keep warm.

Mix the cornflour with a little cold water to form a smooth paste and stir it into the stock. Bring to the boil, stirring continuously. Adjust seasoning if necessary. Strain the gravy before serving.

COOKING TIME
High/15-lb. pressure beef 15 minutes
Reduce pressure with cold water
      vegetables added 10 minutes
Reduce pressure slowly
Fixed 7$\frac{1}{2}$-lb. pressure beef 30 minutes
      vegetables added 20 minutes

Bolognese Sauce

 Serves 4–6

INGREDIENTS

	Imperial	Metric	American
Cooking oil	*2 tbsp.*	*2 tbsp.*	*2 tbsp.*
Large onions, chopped	*2*	*2*	*2*
Clove garlic, crushed	*1*	*1*	*1*
Bacon (streaky), chopped	*4 oz.*	*100 g.*	*$\frac{1}{4}$ lb.*
Minced beef/ hamburger	*1 lb.*	*450 g.*	*1 lb.*
Can tomatoes	*14 oz.*	*397 g.*	*1 med.*
Beef stock	*$\frac{1}{2}$ pt*	*300 ml.*	*1$\frac{1}{4}$ cups*
(If 7$\frac{1}{2}$-lb. pressure)	*$\frac{3}{4}$ pt*	*400 ml.*	*2 cups*
Salt and pepper			

Heat the oil in the open pressure cooker and in it sauté the onions, garlic and bacon gently for about 2 minutes. Add the minced beef and cook for a further few minutes till the mince is lightly browned. Add the remaining ingredients, bring to pressure and cook for given time. Reduce pressure.

If necessary, return the open pressure cooker to the heat and cook the sauce for a few minutes to reduce and thicken it. Serve with buttered spaghetti.

COOKING TIME
High/15-lb. pressure 15 minutes
Reduce pressure slowly
Fixed 7$\frac{1}{2}$-lb. pressure 30 minutes

TO FREEZE
Omit garlic. Pack into rigid polythene container, leaving headspace; cover and freeze. Stir in garlic or season well with garlic salt on reheating.

Barbecued Beef and Noodles

 Serves 4

INGREDIENTS	Imperial	Metric	American
Stewing steak, sliced thinly	2 lb.	1 kg.	2 lb.
Cooking oil	2 tbsp.	2 tbsp.	2 tbsp.
Worcestershire sauce	4 tbsp.	4 tbsp.	4 tbsp.
Tomato ketchup	4 tbsp.	4 tbsp.	4 tbsp.
Vinegar	1 tbsp.	1 tbsp.	1 tbsp.
Sugar	2 tsp.	2 tsp.	2 tsp.
Dry mustard	1 tsp.	1 tsp.	1 tsp.
Paprika	$\frac{1}{2}$ tsp.	$\frac{1}{2}$ tsp.	$\frac{1}{2}$ tsp.
Salt	1 tsp.	1 tsp.	1 tsp.
Small onion, chopped	1	1	1
Beef stock	1 pt	550 ml.	$2\frac{1}{2}$ cups
Noodles	4 oz.	100 g.	$\frac{1}{4}$ lb.
Salted peanuts	2 oz.	50 g.	2 tbsp.

Heat the oil in the open pressure cooker and lightly brown the meat. Add all ingredients except noodles and peanuts and mix well. Bring to pressure and cook for given time. Reduce pressure.

Add the noodles to the beef mixture, bring to pressure again and cook for given time. Reduce pressure. Arrange beef and noodles on a serving dish and sprinkle salted peanuts over them.

COOKING TIME
High/15-lb. pressure meat and sauce 11 minutes
Reduce pressure with cold water
    noodles added 4 minutes
Reduce pressure slowly
Fixed $7\frac{1}{2}$-lb. pressure meat and sauce 22 minutes
    noodles added 8 minutes
    Note: Once the noodles have been added, take care not to overcook this dish.

Paprika Lamb Cutlets

 Serves 4

INGREDIENTS	Imperial	Metric	American
Butter	1 oz.	25 g.	2 tbsp.
Lamb cutlets	8	8	8
Onion, chopped	1	1	1
Small green pepper, de-seeded and chopped	1	1	1
Paprika pepper	3 tsp.	3 tsp.	3 tsp.
Chicken stock	½ pt.	300 ml.	1¼ cups
(If 7½-lb. pressure)	¾ pt	400 ml.	2 cups
Bay leaf			
Tomato purée/paste	2 tbsp.	2 tbsp.	2 tbsp.
Sugar	2 tsp.	2 tsp.	2 tsp.
Salt and pepper			
Carrots, quartered	4	4	4
New potatoes	16	16	16
Butter, Chopped parsley			
Cornflour or cornstarch	2 tbsp.	2 tbsp.	2 tbsp.

Heat the butter in the open pressure cooker and brown the cutlets quickly. Add the onion, green pepper, paprika pepper, chicken stock, bay leaf, tomato purée and sugar. Season to taste. Place the trivet on the cutlets and arrange the vegetables on top. Season with salt and pepper. Bring to pressure and cook for given time. Reduce pressure. Arrange the vegetables on a serving dish, dot with butter and sprinkle with chopped parsley. Keep them warm.

Arrange the cutlets on a serving dish and keep them warm. Mix the cornflour with a little cold water to form a smooth paste and add it to the paprika sauce. Bring to the boil, stirring well.

COOKING TIME
High/15-lb. pressure 10 minutes
Reduce pressure with cold water
Fixed 7½-lb. pressure 20 minutes

Minty Lamb Rolls

 Serves 4

INGREDIENTS	Imperial	Metric	American
White breadcrumbs	4 oz.	100 g.	2 cups
Chopped onion	2 tbsp.	2 tbsp.	2 tbsp.
Chopped fresh mint	1 tsp.	1 tsp.	1 tsp.
Salt and pepper			
Egg, beaten	1	1	1
Breast of lamb, boned	2 lb.	1 kg.	2 lb.
Cooking oil	1 tbsp.	1 tbsp.	1 tbsp.
Butter	1 tbsp.	1 tbsp.	1 tbsp.
Water	$\frac{1}{2}$ pt	300 ml.	$1\frac{1}{4}$ cups
(If 7½-lb. pressure)	$\frac{3}{4}$ pt	400 ml.	2 cups
Bay leaf			
Black peppercorns	6	6	6
Carrot, chopped	1	1	1
Flour	2 tbsp.	2 tbsp.	2 tbsp.
Gravy browning or brown food colouring			

Mix together the breadcrumbs, onion and mint. Season well and bind the mixture with the beaten egg. Trim excess fat off the lamb and spread the stuffing evenly over the inner surface. Roll it up tightly and secure with four cocktail sticks. Slice the lamb into four rolls, cutting between the cocktail sticks. Season well with salt and pepper.

Heat the oil and butter in the open pressure cooker and brown the meat well on all sides. Remove from the pressure cooker. If you have the bones from the lamb breast, place them in the open pressure cooker along with the water, bay leaf, peppercorns and carrot. Place the trivet on top of the bones, then arrange the lamb rolls on the trivet. Bring to pressure and cook for given time. Reduce pressure. Place the lamb on a serving dish and keep it warm. Strain the stock and discard the bones etc.

Mix the flour with a little cold water to form a smooth paste. Return the stock to the open pressure cooker and stir in the flour mixture. Bring to the boil, stirring well, and colour as desired. Pour a little gravy over and around the lamb and serve the rest separately.

COOKING TIME
High/15-lb. pressure 15 minutes
Reduce pressure with cold water
Fixed 7½-lb. pressure 30 minutes

TO FREEZE
Pack the lamb rolls and sauce separately and freeze. Pour gravy over the lamb to reheat.

Note: Make sure the lamb is tightly rolled and the cocktail sticks secure. Use a sharp knife to slice it or the rolls may come adrift.

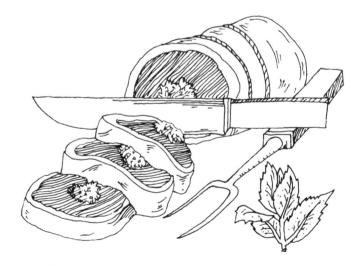

Rich Lamb Casserole

 Serves 4–6

INGREDIENTS

	Imperial	Metric	American
Red kidney beans	4 oz.	100 g.	¼ lb.
Leg lamb, cut into cubes	2-lb.	1-kg.	2-lb.
Seasoned flour			
Cooking oil	2 tbsp.	2 tbsp.	2 tbsp.
Onion stock			
Tomatoes, skinned	8 oz.	225 g.	½ lb.
Tomato purée/paste	1 tbsp.	1 tbsp.	1 tbsp.
Cloves garlic, crushed	2	2	2
Good pinch dried marjoram			
Red pepper, de-seeded and sliced	1	1	1

Place the kidney beans in a bowl, cover them with boiling water, and leave to stand for 1 hour. Toss the lamb in seasoned flour. Heat the oil in the open pressure cooker and in it brown the meat lightly. Remove meat from the pressure cooker with a draining spoon. Drain the beans and make up the soaking liquid to ½ pt/300 ml./1¼ cups with onion stock (¾ pt/400 ml./2 cups for fixed 7½-lb. pressure). Add the beans and stock to the pressure cooker. Bring to pressure and cook for given time. Reduce pressure.

Stir the lamb and all remaining ingredients into the bean mixture, seasoning well. Bring to pressure and cook for given time. Reduce pressure.

COOKING TIME

High/15-lb. pressure beans and stock 10 minutes
Reduce pressure with cold water
    lamb added 15 minutes
Reduce pressure slowly
Fixed 7½-lb. pressure beans and stock 20 minutes
    lamb added 25 minutes

Lamb Cutlets Italian Style

 Serves 4

INGREDIENTS

	Imperial	Metric	American
Cooking oil	2 tbsp.	2 tbsp.	2 tbsp.
Salt and pepper			
Lamb cutlets	8	8	8
Large onion, chopped	1	1	1
Clove garlic, crushed	1	1	1
Large carrot, chopped	1	1	1
Canned tomatoes	14-oz.	397-g.	Med.
Water, if 7½-lb. pressure	¼ pt	150 ml.	⅔ cup
Dried oregano	1 tsp.	1 tsp.	1 tsp.
Flour	2 tbsp.	2 tbsp.	2 tbsp.

Heat the oil in the open pressure cooker and in it brown the well-seasoned cutlets on each side. Remove from pressure cooker. In the same oil sauté the onion, garlic and carrot for 2–3 minutes. Add the tomatoes (including juice), water (if fixed 7½-lb. pressure) and oregano. Place the trivet on top of the vegetables and arrange the cutlets on the trivet. Bring to pressure and cook for given time. Reduce pressure. Transfer the cutlets to a serving dish and keep them warm. Mix the flour with a little cold water to form a smooth paste and stir it into the sauce. Bring to the boil, stirring continuously. Pour the sauce over the cutlets and serve.

COOKING TIME

High/15-lb. pressure 10 minutes
Reduce pressure with cold water
Fixed 7½-lb. pressure 20 minutes

Redcurrant Lamb Roll

Serves 4

INGREDIENTS	Imperial	Metric	American
Onion, finely chopped	2 tbsp.	2 tbsp.	2 tbsp.
White breadcrumbs	1½ oz.	40 g.	¾–1 cup
Dried mixed herbs	2 tsp.	2 tsp.	2 tsp.
Salt and pepper			
Egg, beaten	1	1	1
Loin lamb, boned	2 lb.	1 kg.	2 lb.
Seasoned flour			
Cooking oil	2 tbsp.	2 tbsp.	2 tbsp.
Carrots, sliced thickly	8 oz.	225 g.	½ lb.
Water	½ pt	300 ml.	1¼ cups
(If 7½-lb. pressure)	¾ pt	400 ml.	2 cups
Medium onion, sliced	1	1	1
Bouquet garni			
Cornflour/cornstarch	2 tbsp.	2 tbsp.	2 tbsp.
Red-currant jelly	2 tbsp.	2 tbsp.	2 tbsp.

Mix together the onion, breadcrumbs and herbs. Season well and bind with a little beaten egg. Spread the stuffing over the inner surface of the lamb, roll it up tightly and secure with string. Brush remaining egg over the lamb, then coat well with seasoned flour. Heat the oil in the open pressure cooker and brown the lamb well on all sides and both ends. Lift out. In the same oil, sauté the carrots gently till golden brown. Lift out. If you have the bones from the lamb, arrange these in the pressure cooker. Add the water, onion and bouquet garni. Position the trivet on top of the bones, then the lamb on the trivet. Bring to pressure and cook for given time. Reduce pressure.

Place the carrots around the lamb and bring to pressure again for given time. Reduce pressure.

Arrange lamb and vegetables on a serving dish. Strain the stock and return the liquid to the open pressure cooker. Mix the flour with a little cold water to form a smooth paste and stir it into the stock. Bring to the boil, stirring well. Add the red-currant jelly and allow it to melt. Pour a little over the lamb and serve the remainder separately.

COOKING TIME
High/15-lb. pressure lamb 20 minutes
Reduce pressure with cold water
    carrots added 5 minutes
Reduce pressure slowly
Fixed 7½-lb. pressure lamb 40 minutes
    carrots added 10 minutes

Traditional Lamb Hot Pot

Serves 4

INGREDIENTS	Imperial	Metric	American
Middle neck lamb chops	8	8	8
Cooking oil	2 tbsp.	2 tbsp.	2 tbsp.
Onions, sliced	8 oz.	225 g.	$\frac{1}{2}$ lb.
Carrots, sliced	4 oz.	100 g.	$\frac{1}{4}$ lb.
Potatoes, sliced	1 lb.	450 g.	1 lb.
Salt and pepper			
Stock	$\frac{3}{4}$ pt	400 ml.	2 cups
(If 7$\frac{1}{2}$lb. pressure)	1 pt	550 ml.	2$\frac{1}{2}$ cups

Trim excess fat off chops. Heat the cooking oil in the open pressure cooker and brown the chops on all sides. Add the onions, carrots and potatoes and cook gently for a further 3–4 minutes. Season well and add stock. Bring to pressure and cook for given time. Reduce pressure.

If necessary remove some of the surface fat with kitchen paper. Arrange the chops, vegetables and stock in a serving dish, finishing with a layer of potatoes. Brown under a hot grill before serving.

COOKING TIME
High/15-lb. pressure 15 minutes
Reduce pressure slowly
Fixed 7$\frac{1}{2}$-lb. pressure 30 minutes

Somerset Pork

 Serves 4

INGREDIENTS	Imperial	Metric	American
Loin pork, rind removed	2 lb.	1 kg.	2 lb.
Salt and pepper			
Cloves	8	8	8
Cooking oil	1 tbsp.	1 tbsp.	1 tbsp.
Large leek, sliced	1	1	1
Large carrots, sliced	2	2	2
Celery, sliced	2 sticks	2 sticks	2 stalks
Dry cider	¾ pt	400 ml.	2 cups
(If 7½-lb. pressure)	1 pt	550 ml.	2½ cups
Bay leaf			
Flour	3 tbsp.	3 tbsp.	3 tbsp.

Season the pork well with salt and pepper. Stick the cloves into the fat side of the meat. Heat the oil in the open pressure cooker and brown the pork on all sides. Remove from pressure cooker. In the same oil sauté the vegetables gently till golden brown, seasoning well. Remove from pressure cooker. Pour the cider on to any remaining oil and add the bay leaf. Position the trivet and place the pork on top. Bring to pressure and cook for given time. Reduce pressure. Arrange the vegetables round the pork and bring to pressure again for given time. Reduce pressure. Put the pork and vegetables on a serving dish; keep them warm. Remove bay leaf. Mix the flour with a little cold water to form a smooth paste and stir it into the sauce. Bring to the boil, stirring continuously. Adjust seasoning if necessary. Serve the sauce separately.

COOKING TIME
High/15-lb. pressure meat 25 minutes
Reduce pressure with cold water
vegetables added 5 minutes
Reduce pressure slowly
Fixed 7½-lb. pressure meat 45 minutes
vegetables added 10 minutes

Lemon Pork

 Serves 4

INGREDIENTS	Imperial	Metric	American
Pork, cut into cubes	1½ lb.	700 g.	1½ lb.
Cooking oil	3 tbsp.	3 tbsp.	3 tbsp.
Grated rind and juice 1 lemon			
Dried tarragon	1–1½ tsp.	1–1½ tsp.	1–1½ tsp.
Freshly-ground black pepper	½ tsp.	½ tsp.	½ tsp.
Large carrots, cut up	3	3	3
Dry cider	½ pt	300 ml.	1¼ cups
(If 7½-lb. pressure)	¾ pt	400 ml.	2 cups
Spring onions, chopped	6–8	6–8	6–8
Cornflour/cornstarch	2 tbsp.	2 tbsp.	2 tbsp.

Place the pork in a shallow bowl. Mix together the oil, lemon rind and juice, tarragon and black pepper. Pour the mixture over the pork pieces, coating well. Marinate for 1–2 hours, turning the pork occasionally.

Place the open pressure cooker on the heat and pour in the pork and marinade. Toss the pork for a few minutes till it is lightly browned, then add the carrots and cook for a further minute. Add the cider, bring to pressure and cook for given time. Reduce pressure.

Stir in the chopped onions. Mix the cornflour with a little cold water to form a smooth paste and stir into the pork. Bring to the boil, stirring continuously. Serve immediately.

COOKING TIME
High/15-lb. pressure 20 minutes
Reduce pressure slowly
Fixed 7½-lb. pressure 35 minutes

Pork Stroganoff

 Serves 4

INGREDIENTS	Imperial	Metric	American
Butter	1 oz.	25 g.	2 tbsp.
Pork, cut into cubes	1½ lb.	700 g.	1½ lb.
Tomatoes, skinned and quartered	4	4	4
Small onions	8	8	8
Button mushrooms	4 oz.	100 g.	¼ lb.
Chicken stock	½ pt	300 ml.	1¼ cups
(If 7½-lb. pressure)	¾ pt	400 ml.	2 cups
Salt and pepper			
Soured cream/yoghurt	¼ pt	150 ml.	⅔ cup
Chopped parsley	1 tbsp.	1 tbsp.	1 tbsp.

Heat the butter in the open pressure cooker and in it brown the pork pieces lightly. Add the tomatoes, whole onions, whole mushrooms and chicken stock. Season well. Bring to pressure and cook for given time. Reduce pressure.

Just before serving, stir in the soured cream and chopped parsley.

COOKING TIME
High/15-lb. pressure 20 minutes
Reduce pressure with cold water
Fixed 7½-lb. pressure 35 minutes

TO FREEZE
Pack in rigid polythene container, cover and freeze. Stir in soured cream and parsley at reheating stage.

Pork Chops with Apple Sauce

 Serves 4

INGREDIENTS	Imperial	Metric	American
Pork chops	4	4	4
Salt and pepper			
Cooking oil	1 tbsp.	1 tbsp.	1 tbsp.
Eating apples, peeled, cored and chopped	2	2	2
Celery, chopped	2 sticks	2 sticks	2 stalks
Small onion, chopped	1	1	1
Water	$\frac{1}{2}$ pt	300 ml.	$1\frac{1}{4}$ cups
(If $7\frac{1}{2}$-lb. pressure)	$\frac{3}{4}$ pt	400 ml.	2 cups
Good pinch dried sage			
Baby carrots	12	12	12
Butter	1 tbsp.	1 tbsp.	1 tbsp.
Flour	1 tbsp.	1 tbsp.	1 tbsp.

Trim excess fat from chops and season well. Heat the oil in the open pressure cooker and in it brown the chops quickly on both sides. Remove from the pressure cooker. In the same oil sauté the apples, celery and onion gently for 2–3 minutes, then add the water and sage. Place the trivet on top of the apple mixture. Arrange the chops and whole carrots on the trivet. Bring to pressure and cook for given time. Reduce pressure.

Arrange the chops and carrots on a serving dish and keep them warm. Liquidize or sieve the apple sauce. Melt the butter in the open pressure cooker and add the flour to form a *roux*. Slowly stir in the apple mixture and bring to the boil. Adjust seasoning if necessary.

COOKING TIME
High/15-lb. pressure 10 minutes
Reduce pressure with cold water
Fixed $7\frac{1}{2}$-lb. pressure 20 minutes

Veal and Mushroom Cream

 Serves 4

INGREDIENTS	Imperial	Metric	American
Pie veal, cut into cubes	1½ lb.	700 g.	1½ lb.
Seasoned flour			
Butter	2 oz.	50 g.	¼ cup
Onion, chopped	1	1	1
Clove garlic, crushed (optional)	1	1	1
Pinch dried thyme			
Dry cider	½ pt	300 ml.	1¼ cups
(If 7½-lb. pressure)	¾ pt	400 ml.	2 cups
Salt and pepper			
Mushrooms, sliced	8 oz.	225 g.	½ lb.
Single or thin cream	6 fl.-oz.	175-ml.	⅔ cup
Watercress			

Coat the veal with seasoned flour. Heat the butter in the open pressure cooker and in it lightly brown the veal. Add the onion and garlic and cook for a further minute. Add the thyme, cider and seasoning, then stir in the mushrooms. Bring to pressure and cook for given time. Reduce pressure. Stir in the cream just before serving. Garnish with watercress.

COOKING TIME
High/15-lb. pressure 12 minutes
Reduce pressure slowly
Fixed 7½-lb. pressure 25 minutes

TO FREEZE
Omit garlic and cream (stir them in at reheating stage). Pack into rigid polythene container, cover and freeze.

Veal Roll with Herbs

 Serves 4

INGREDIENTS

	Imperial	Metric	American
Loin veal, boned	*2½ lb.*	*1.1 kg.*	*2½ lb.*
Cooking oil	*2 tbsp.*	*2 tbsp.*	*2 tbsp.*
Pinch each of thyme, basil, cloves and mace			
Juice 1 lemon			
Small potatoes	*8*	*8*	*8*
Small carrots	*4*	*4*	*4*
Small onions	*4*	*4*	*4*
Salt and pepper			
Onion stock cube	*1*	*1*	*1*
Water	*¾ pt*	*400 ml.*	*2 cups*
(If 7½-lb. pressure)	*1 pt*	*550 ml.*	*2½ cups*
Flour	*3 tbsp.*	*3 tbsp.*	*3 tbsp.*

Roll the veal tightly and tie securely with string. Mix together half of the cooking oil with the thyme, basil, cloves, mace and lemon juice. Brush the mixture all over the veal roll. Heat the remaining oil in the open pressure cooker and in it brown the meat on all sides and both ends. Remove from the pressure cooker. In the same oil, sauté the whole vegetables till lightly browned, seasoning well. Remove from the pressure cooker. Dissolve the stock cube in the water and pour it into the pressure cooker. Place trivet in position with the veal roll on top. Pour any remaining herb/lemon mixture over the veal, bring to pressure and cook for given time. Reduce pressure.

Put the vegetables around the veal and bring to pressure again for given time. Reduce pressure.

Slice the veal and arrange it on a serving dish with the vegetables. Keep it warm. Mix the flour with a little cold water to form a smooth paste and stir this into the sauce. Bring to the boil, stirring

well. Pour a little over the veal slices and serve the rest separately.

COOKING TIME

High/15-lb. pressure meat 20 minutes
Reduce pressure with cold water
    vegetables added 7 minutes
Reduce pressure slowly
Fixed 7½-lb. pressure meat 35 minutes
    vegetables added 15 minutes

TO FREEZE

Pack leftover slices of the veal with sauce poured over them in a foil tray. Cover and freeze.

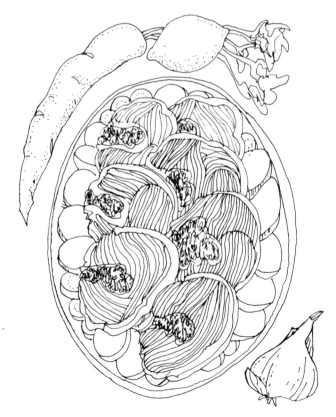

POULTRY AND GAME

Poultry and game are ideally suited to pressure-cooking. Even the tougher boiling fowls and older game birds are beautifully tenderized when cooked under pressure. Poultry, notably turkey, tends to dry out during cooking, but in a pressure cooker the result is always moist. Though whole turkey will be too large for your pressure cooker, turkey joints are most suitable.

POULTRY, GAME AND FREEZING

Frozen poultry should always be thawed completely.

Pressure-cooked poultry and game dishes can of course be frozen. Special instructions are given in the recipes where freezing is recommended.

To reheat frozen cooked poultry or game dishes, follow the instructions for reheating frozen meat dishes on page 26.

CHECKPOINTS FOR POULTRY AND GAME

Remember to fill the pressure cooker no more than half full with casserole-type dishes.

Birds up to 3½ lb./1.6 kg. can be cooked successfully in the pressure cooker. Above this weight, cooking tends to be uneven. Also, enough space must be allowed for the steam to circulate.

Truss whole birds before pressure cooking.

Cooking times for poultry depend on the type of bird (roasting or boiling for example) and its weight. The table opposite gives cooking times. Stuffed birds should be weighed stuffed. Cooking times for game depend on its weight/age.

The minimum amount of liquid recommended by the manufacturer must be included. When cooking whole birds, the quantity of liquid (stock, water, wine, cider, fruit juice etc.) depends on the cooking time. Check the manufacturers' instructions.

Poultry and game are best sautéed (lightly fried) before pressure-cooking.

The trivet is used where the poultry or game is to be cooked in steam. It is not used for casserole-type dishes.

Thickening agents are best added after cooking to obtain the correct consistency.

To serve vegetables with poultry, reduce pressure a few minutes before the end of cooking, add the vegetables and bring to pressure again for the required time.

When adapting your own recipes for pressure cooking less liquid than normal will be needed.

The following times for pressure-cooking poultry and game are for High/15-lb. pressure. If your pressure cooker is fixed at 7½-lb., just double the times given below and follow the manufacturers' instructions on the amount of liquid to use.

Poultry and Game		Cooking time at High/15-lb. pressure
Chicken:		
Poussin,	halved	7 minutes
	joints	4 minutes
Roasting,	whole	5 minutes per 1 lb./450 g.
	joints	5–7 minutes (depending on size)
Boiling,	whole	10 minutes per 1 lb./450 g.
	joints	10–15 minutes (depending on size)
Turkey,	joints	10 minutes
Duck,	whole	12–15 minutes per 1 lb./450 g.
	joints	12 minutes
Grouse		10 minutes
Pigeons		10 minutes
Hare,	joints	40 minutes
Rabbit,	joints	15 minutes
Pheasant,	whole	7–10 minutes (depending on age)
Partridge		
	joints	5–7 minutes (depending on age)

Chicken Treat

 Serves 4

INGREDIENTS

	Imperial	Metric	American
Butter	2 oz.	50 g.	$\frac{1}{4}$ cup
Chicken joints	4	4	4
Medium onion, chopped	1	1	1
Medium green pepper, de-seeded and sliced	1	1	1
Garlic sausage, cut into thin strips	4 oz.	100 g.	$\frac{1}{4}$ lb.
Dry cider	$\frac{3}{4}$ pt.	400 ml.	2 cups
Salt and Pepper			
Cornflour/cornstarch	3 tbsp.	3 tbsp.	3 tbsp.

Heat the butter in the open pressure cooker and in it brown the chicken joints on all sides. Remove from the pressure cooker. In the same butter, gently sauté the onion and green pepper for 2 minutes. Replace the chicken joints and scatter the strips of garlic sausage over them. Add the cider and season well. Bring to pressure and cook for given time. Reduce pressure. Mix the cornflour with a little cold water to form a smooth paste and stir it into the chicken mixture. Bring to the boil. Serve with plenty of green salad.

COOKING TIME
High/15-lb. pressure 7 minutes
Reduce pressure with cold water
Fixed 7$\frac{1}{2}$-lb. pressure 15 minutes

TO FREEZE
Omit garlic sausage. Pack into rigid polythene container, cover and freeze. Stir in the garlic sausage strips at reheating stage.

Curried Chicken with Sweetcorn

 Serves 4

INGREDIENTS

	Imperial	Metric	American
Chicken thighs	8	8	8
Salt and pepper			
Butter	2 oz.	50 g.	$\frac{1}{4}$ cup
Medium onion, diced	1	1	1
Medium carrot, diced	1	1	1
Packet frozen sweet corn	8 oz.	226 g.	$\frac{1}{2}$ lb.
Curry powder (or to taste)	3 tsp.	3 tsp.	3 tsp.
Chicken stock	$\frac{1}{2}$ pt	300 ml.	1$\frac{1}{4}$ cups
Flour	2-3 tbsp.	2-3 tbsp.	2-3 tbsp.
Chopped parsley			

Season the chicken well with salt and pepper. Heat the butter in the open pressure cooker and in it brown the chicken on all sides. Add the onion and carrot and cook gently for a further 1 minute, stirring well. Add the frozen sweet corn, curry powder and stock. Bring to pressure and cook for given time. Reduce pressure. Mix the flour with a little cold water to form a smooth paste. Stir it into the chicken mixture and bring to the boil, stirring continuously. Garnish with chopped parsley and serve.

COOKING TIME
High/15-lb. pressure 7 minutes
Reduce pressure with cold water
Fixed 7$\frac{1}{2}$-lb. pressure 10 minutes

TO FREEZE
Omit curry powder and parsley and add at reheating stage.

Cyprus Chicken

 Serves 4

INGREDIENTS	Imperial	Metric	American
Butter	2 oz.	50 g.	$\frac{1}{4}$ cup
Chicken joints	4	4	4
Medium onion, chopped	1	1	1
Mushrooms, sliced	8 oz.	225 g.	$\frac{1}{2}$ lb.
Medium dry sherry	$\frac{1}{4}$ pt	150 ml.	$\frac{2}{3}$ cup
(If $7\frac{1}{2}$-lb. pressure)	$\frac{1}{3}$ pt	200 ml.	1 cup
Salt			
Black pepper			
Double thick cream	$\frac{1}{2}$ pt	225 ml.	$1\frac{1}{4}$ cups
Paprika	$\frac{1}{2}$–1 tsp.	$\frac{1}{2}$–1 tsp.	$\frac{1}{2}$–1 tsp.
Chopped parsley	2 tbsp.	2 tbsp.	2 tbsp.

Heat the butter in the open pressure cooker and brown the chicken joints well on all sides. Remove. In the same butter sauté the onions gently for 2–3 minutes. Stir in the mushrooms and sherry and season with salt and black pepper. Bring to pressure and cook for given time. Reduce pressure. Lift the chicken joints on to a serving dish and keep warm. Stir the remaining ingredients into the sherry mixture. Adjust seasoning if necessary then reheat (without boiling) and pour over the chicken.

COOKING TIME
High/15-lb. pressure 7 minutes
Reduce pressure with cold water
Fixed $7\frac{1}{2}$-lb. pressure 15 minutes

TO FREEZE
Omit last three ingredients. Pack in rigid polythene container, cover and freeze. Thaw in room temperature then stir in the cream, paprika and parsley on reheating.

Lemon Chicken

 Serves 4–6

INGREDIENTS	Imperial	Metric	American
Boiling fowl	1	1	1
Juice 1 lemon			
Butter	1 oz.	25 g.	2 tbsp.
Small onions	8 oz.	225 g.	½ lb.
Carrots	8 oz.	225 g.	½ lb.
Bay leaves	2	2	2
Black peppercorns	6	6	6
Chicken stock	¾ pt	400 ml.	2 cups
(If 7½-lb. pressure)	1 pt	550 ml.	2½ cups
Egg	1	1	1
Double or thick cream	4 tbsp.	4 tbsp.	4 tbsp.
Sherry	2 tbsp.	2 tbsp.	2 tbsp.
Blanched almonds	2 oz.	50 g.	2 tbsp.

Sprinkle the bird with the lemon juice. Heat the butter in the open pressure cooker and in it brown the chicken on all sides. Add the whole onions and carrots, bay leaves, peppercorns and chicken stock. Bring to pressure and cook for given time. Reduce pressure.

Place the chicken on a serving dish and arrange the vegetables around. Keep it warm. Discard bay leaves and peppercorns. Beat together the egg and cream and gradually add the hot stock, stirring all the time till it is thick but smooth. Stir in the sherry and almonds. Pour a little sauce over the chicken and vegetables and serve the remainder separately.

COOKING TIME
High/15-lb. pressure 10 minutes per 1 lb./450 g.
Reduce pressure with cold water
Fixed 7½-lb. pressure 15 minutes per 1 lb./450 g.

Chicken Italienne

 Serves 4

INGREDIENTS

	Imperial	Metric	American
Butter	2 oz.	50 g.	¼ cup
Chicken thighs	8	8	8
Garlic cloves, crushed	2	2	2
Onions, chopped	2	2	2
Streaky bacon, chopped	4 oz.	100 g.	¼ lb.
Tomato purée or paste	4 tbsp.	4 tbsp.	4 tbsp.
Chicken stock	¾ pt	400 ml.	2 cups
Tomatoes, skinned and sliced	4	4	4
Mushrooms, sliced	4 oz.	100 g.	¼ lb.
Dried oregano	1 tsp.	1 tsp.	1 tsp.
Salt and pepper			
Flour	2 tbsp.	2 tbsp.	2 tbsp.

Heat the butter in the open pressure cooker and in it brown the chicken on all sides. Remove it from the pressure cooker. In the same butter, sauté the garlic, onions and bacon gently for about 2 minutes. Stir in the tomatoes, mushrooms, tomato purée, chicken stock, oregano and seasoning. Return the chicken to pressure cooker, bring to pressure and cook for given time. Reduce pressure.

Mix the flour with a little cold water to form a smooth paste and stir it into the chicken. Bring to the boil, stirring continuously.

COOKING TIME
High/15-lb. pressure 7 minutes
Reduce pressure with cold water
Fixed 7½-lb. pressure 10 minutes

TO FREEZE
Omit garlic. Pack it in rigid polythene container, cover and freeze. Add garlic at reheating stage, or season with garlic salt.

Chicken with Herbs

 Serves 4

INGREDIENTS

	Imperial	Metric	American
Butter	1 oz.	25 g.	2 tbsp.
Cooking oil	1 tbsp.	1 tbsp.	1 tbsp.
Boiling fowl	1	1	1
Salt and pepper			
Onion, chopped	1	1	1
White wine	½ pt	300 ml.	1¼ cups
Chicken stock	¼ pt	150 ml.	⅔ cup
(If 7½-lb. pressure)	½ pt	300 ml.	1¼ cups
Dried rosemary	½ tsp.	½ tsp.	½ tsp.
Dried tarragon	½ tsp.	½ tsp.	½ tsp.
Cornflour/cornstarch	2 tbsp.	2 tbsp.	2 tbsp.

Heat the butter and oil in the open pressure cooker and in it brown the seasoned chicken on all sides. Remove from pressure cooker. In the same fat, sauté the onion gently for 1–2 minutes. Add the white wine and chicken stock.

Sprinkle the herbs over the chicken and return it to the pressure cooker. Bring to pressure and cook for given time. Reduce pressure.

Place the chicken on a serving dish and keep it warm. Mix the cornflour with a little cold water to form a smooth paste and stir this into the sauce. Bring to the boil, stirring continuously. Pour a little sauce around the chicken and serve the rest separately.

COOKING TIME
High/15-lb. pressure 10 minutes per lb./450 g.
Reduce pressure with cold water
Fixed 7½-lb. pressure 15 minutes per lb/450 g.

Creamy Chicken Casserole

Serves 4

INGREDIENTS

	Imperial	Metric	American
Butter beans	8 oz.	225 g.	½ lb.
Butter	2 oz.	50 g.	¼ cup
Cooking oil	2 tbsp.	2 tbsp.	2 tbsp.
Chicken joints	4	4	4
Medium onions, chopped	2	2	2
Carrots, sliced	8 oz.	225 g.	½ lb.
Chicken stock			
Good pinch dried basil			
Salt and pepper			
Canned condensed celery soup	10½-oz.	298 g.	medium

Place the butter beans in a dish and cover them with boiling water. Cover with a plate and leave for 1 hour. Heat the butter and cooking oil in the open pressure cooker and in it brown the chicken joints on all sides. Remove chicken from the pressure cooker and set it to one side. In the same butter, sauté the onions and carrots gently for 2–3 minutes. Make up the soaking liquid from the butter beans to ½ pt/300 ml./1¼ cups with chicken stock (¾ pt/400 ml./2 cups if fixed 7½-lb. pressure) and add it to the pressure cooker. Stir in the butter beans, basil and seasoning. Bring to pressure and cook for given time. Reduce pressure.

Add the chicken pieces to the butter bean mixture in the pressure cooker. Bring to pressure again and cook for given time. Reduce pressure.

Carefully stir in the condensed soup, adjusting seasoning if necessary. Reheat and serve.

COOKING TIME
High/15-lb. pressure 13 minutes
Reduce pressure slowly
    chicken added 7 minutes
Reduce pressure slowly
Fixed 7½-lb. pressure 25 minutes
    chicken added 10 minutes

TO FREEZE
Pack in rigid polythene container, cover and freeze. Extra thickening may be needed after freezing. Thaw at room temperature and reheat gently.

Cherried Chicken

Serves 4

INGREDIENTS

	Imperial	Metric	American
Chicken joints	4	4	4
Salt and pepper			
Cooking oil	2 tbsp.	2 tbsp.	2 tbsp.
Chicken stock	½ pt	300 ml.	1¼ cups
Canned black cherries	15 oz.	425 g.	1 lb.
Cornflour or Cornstarch	2–3 tbsp.	2–3 tbsp.	2–3 tbsp.

Season the chicken joints with salt and pepper. Heat the oil in the open pressure cooker and in it brown the chicken on all sides. Add the stock and the syrup from the black cherries. Bring to pressure and cook for given time. Reduce pressure.

Arrange the chicken joints on a serving dish. Add the cherries to the sauce in the pressure cooker. Mix the cornflour with a little cold water to form a smooth paste and add it to the cherry sauce. Bring to the boil, stirring continuously. Pour the sauce around chicken to serve. Garnish with watercress if liked.

COOKING TIME
High/15-lb. pressure 7 minutes
Reduce pressure with cold water
Fixed 7½-lb. pressure 15 minutes

Turkey Marengo

 Serves 4

INGREDIENTS

	Imperial	Metric	American
Turkey joints	4	4	4
Salt and pepper			
Cooking oil	2 tbsp.	2 tbsp.	2 tbsp.
Clove garlic, crushed	1	1	1
Large onion, sliced	1	1	1
Carrots, sliced	2	2	2
Canned tomatoes	14-oz.	396-g.	1-lb.
Chicken stock	$\frac{1}{4}$ pt	150 ml.	$\frac{2}{3}$ cup
Button mushrooms	4 oz.	100 g.	$\frac{1}{4}$ lb.
Bay leaf			
Bouquet garni			
Flour	2 tbsp.	2 tbsp.	2 tbsp.

Season the turkey joints well with salt and pepper. Heat the oil in the open pressure cooker and in it brown the turkey joints on all sides. Remove them from the pressure cooker. In the same oil, sauté the garlic, onion and carrots gently for about 2 minutes. Add the browned turkey joints, tomatoes, chicken stock, mushrooms, bay leaf, and bouquet garni. Bring to pressure and cook for given time. Reduce pressure. Discard bay leaf and bouquet garni. Mix the flour with a little cold water to form a smooth paste. Stir into the turkey mixture and bring to the boil.

COOKING TIME
High/15-lb. pressure 10 minutes
Reduce pressure with cold water
Fixed 7$\frac{1}{2}$-lb. pressure 20 minutes

TO FREEZE
Omit garlic, pour into rigid polythene container, cover and freeze. On reheating, add garlic or season with garlic salt.

Turkey in Apple Juice

 Serves 4

INGREDIENTS	Imperial	Metric	American
Turkey wings	4	4	4
Salt and pepper			
Butter	2 oz.	50 g.	$\frac{1}{4}$ cup
Onion, sliced	1	1	1
Baby carrots	12 oz.	350 g.	$\frac{3}{4}$ lb.
Apple juice	1 pt	550 ml.	$2\frac{1}{2}$ cups
Flour	2 tbsp.	2 tbsp.	2 tbsp.

Season the turkey with salt and pepper. Heat the butter in the open pressure cooker and in it brown the turkey well on all sides. Remove turkey from cooker. In the same butter, sauté the onion and carrots gently for 1–2 minutes. Return turkey to the pressure cooker and add the apple juice. Season well. Bring to pressure and cook for given time. Reduce pressure. Using a draining spoon, transfer the turkey and vegetables to a serving dish. Mix the flour with a little cold water to form a smooth paste and add it to the sauce. Bring to the boil, stirring continuously. Pour a little sauce over the turkey and serve rest separately.

COOKING TIME
High/15-lb. pressure 10 minutes
Reduce pressure with cold water
Fixed 7½-lb. pressure 20 minutes

TO FREEZE
Place turkey and vegetables in a polythene container. Pour the sauce over them, cover and freeze.

Duck in Pineapple

 Serves 4

INGREDIENTS

	Imperial	Metric	American
Cooking oil	2 tbsp.	2 tbsp.	2 tbsp.
Duck joints	4	4	4
Clove garlic, crushed	1	1	1
Ground ginger	½ tsp.	½ tsp.	½ tsp.
Canned pineapple chunks	15-oz.	425-g.	1-lb.
Chicken stock			
Sherry	4 tbsp.	4 tbsp.	⅓ cup
Salt and pepper			
Flour	1 oz.	25 g.	¼ cup

Heat the oil in the open pressure cooker and in it brown the duck joints well on all sides. Add the garlic and ginger. Make pineapple juice up to ½ pt/300 ml./1¼ cups with chicken stock (¾ pt/400 ml. 2 cups if fixed 7½ lb. pressure) and pour it over the duck. Add the sherry and season well. Bring to pressure and cook for given time. Reduce pressure. Remove surface fat with kitchen paper or a metal spoon if necessary. Mix the flour with a little cold water to form a smooth paste and stir it into the duck mixture. Bring to the boil and add pineapple chunks. Reheat and serve.

COOKING TIME
High/15-lb. pressure 12 minutes
Reduce pressure with cold water
Fixed 7½-lb. pressure 25 minutes

Duckling Casserole

 Serves 4

INGREDIENTS

	Imperial	Metric	American
Butter	1 oz.	25 g.	2 tbsp.
Duckling joints	4	4	4
Onions, sliced	2	2	2
Carrots, sliced	2	2	2
Chicken stock	¾ pt	400 ml.	2 cups
Bay leaf			
Chopped parsley	2 tsp.	2 tsp.	2 tsp.
Dried oregano	½ tsp.	½ tsp.	½ tsp.
Salt and pepper			
Cornflour or Cornstarch	3 tbsp.	3 tbsp.	3 tbsp.

Heat the butter in the open pressure cooker and in it brown the duckling joints well on all sides. Remove duckling from pressure cooker. In the same butter, sauté the onions and carrots gently for about 2 minutes. Add the browned duckling joints, chicken stock, bay leaf, parsley, and oregano. Season well, bring to pressure and cook for given time. Reduce pressure. Discard bay leaf. Using kitchen paper or a metal spoon, remove excess fat from the surface of the sauce. Mix the cornflour with a little cold water to form a smooth paste. Add it to the pressure cooker and bring to the boil, stirring continuously.

COOKING TIME
High/15-lb. pressure 12 minutes
Reduce pressure with cold water
Fixed 7½-lb. pressure 25 minutes

TO FREEZE
Pack in rigid polythene container, cover and freeze.

Pheasant with Apple Cream

 Serves 4

INGREDIENTS

	Imperial	Metric	American
Small pheasants	2	2	2
Seasoned flour			
Butter	2 oz.	50 g.	$\frac{1}{4}$ cup
Cooking apples, peeled, cored and sliced	4	4	4
Beef stock	$\frac{1}{2}$ pt	300 ml.	$1\frac{1}{4}$ cups
Double or thick cream	$\frac{1}{4}$ pt.	150 ml.	$\frac{2}{3}$ cup
Watercress			

Coat the pheasants with seasoned flour. Heat the butter in the open pressure cooker and in it brown the pheasant on all sides. Lift them out. In the same butter, sauté the apples gently for 2–3 minutes. Replace the pheasants and pour the beef stock around them. Bring to pressure and cook for given time. Reduce pressure.

Place the pheasants on a serving dish and keep them warm. Liquidize or mash the apple mixture and adjust the seasoning if necessary. Stir in the cream. Garnish the pheasants with watercress and serve the sauce separately.

COOKING TIME
High/15-lb. pressure 8 minutes
Reduce pressure with cold water
Fixed 7$\frac{1}{2}$-lb. pressure 16 minutes

Pigeon Ragout

 Serves 4

INGREDIENTS

	Imperial	Metric	American
Butter	2 oz.	50 g.	$\frac{1}{4}$ cup
Small pigeons	4	4	4
Rashers streaky bacon, or slices bacon, chopped	4	4	4
Tomatoes, skinned and sliced	4	4	4
Beef stock	$\frac{3}{4}$ pt	400 ml.	2 cups
Red wine	4 tbsp.	4 tbsp.	4 tbsp.
Salt and pepper			
Flour	1 oz.	25 g.	$\frac{1}{4}$ cup

Heat the butter in the open pressure cooker and in it lightly brown the pigeons on all sides. Remove from pressure cooker. In the same butter, sauté the bacon gently for about 2 minutes, then stir in the tomatoes, beef stock and red wine. Return the pigeons to the pressure cooker and season with salt and pepper. Bring to pressure and cook for given time. Reduce pressure.

Using a draining spoon, lift the pigeons onto a serving dish. Mix the flour with a little cold water to form a smooth paste. Add it to the sauce and bring to the boil, stirring continuously. Adjust seasoning if necessary. Pour the sauce over and around the pigeons and serve with pieces of fried bread.

COOKING TIME
High/15-lb. pressure 10 minutes
Reduce pressure with cold water
Fixed 7$\frac{1}{2}$-lb. pressure 20 minutes

Mustard Rabbit Casserole

 Serves 4

INGREDIENTS

	Imperial	Metric	American
Butter	2 oz.	50 g.	¼ cup
Rabbit joints	1½ lb.	700 g.	1½ lb.
Streaky bacon, chopped	8 oz.	225 g.	½ lb.
Large onions, chopped	3	3	3
Chicken stock	1 pt	500 ml.	2½ cups
Salt and pepper			
Bouquet garni			
French mustard	1 tbsp.	1 tbsp.	1 tbsp.
Flour	3 tbsp.	3 tbsp.	3 tbsp.

Heat the butter in the open pressure cooker and in it lightly brown the rabbit joints. Lift them out. In the same butter, sauté the bacon and onions for 2–3 minutes. Replace the rabbit and add the chicken stock, seasoning, bouquet garni and mustard. Bring to pressure and cook for given time. Reduce pressure. Mix the flour with a little cold water to form a smooth paste and stir it into the casserole. Bring to the boil, stirring well.

COOKING TIME
High/15-lb. pressure 15 minutes
Reduce pressure with cold water
Fixed 7½-lb. pressure 30 minutes

TO FREEZE
Pack in rigid polythene container, cover and freeze.

Rabbit in Orange

 Serves 4

INGREDIENTS

	Imperial	Metric	American
Butter	2 oz.	50 g.	¼ cup
Rabbit joints	1½ lb.	700 g.	1½ lb.
Medium onion, chopped	1	1	1
Concentrated orange juice	3 fl. oz.	75 ml.	½ cup
Water	¾ pt	400 ml.	2 cups
Chicken stock cube, crumbled	1	1	1
Mushrooms, sliced	4 oz.	100 g.	¼ lb.
Salt and pepper			
Cornflour or Cornstarch	2 tbsp.	2 tbsp.	2 tbsp.

Heat the butter in the open pressure cooker and in it lightly brown the rabbit joints on all sides. Add the onion and cook, stirring for a further 1 minute. Add the concentrated orange juice, water, stock cube and mushrooms. Season well, bring to pressure and cook for given time. Reduce pressure.

Mix the cornflour with a little cold water to form a smooth paste and stir it into the rabbit mixture. Bring to the boil, stirring continuously.

COOKING TIME
High/15-lb. pressure 15 minutes
Reduce pressure with cold water
Fixed 7½-lb. pressure 30 minutes

TO FREEZE
Pack in rigid polythene container, cover and freeze.

FISH

There are several advantages of cooking fish in your pressure cooker. Though the time saving will not be great, since fish is quickly cooked by most methods, I hope you too will appreciate the full flavour of pressure-cooked fish. Hardly any flavour is lost if the minimum amount of liquid is used, and the fish is cooked in the steam. Make sure you retain the flavour and nutritive value by using the cooking liquor to make a delicious accompanying sauce.

Fish keeps its shape very well in the pressure cooker. Whole fish and large pieces are best wrapped in buttered foil to enable easy removal from the pressure cooker.

For me, a big advantage is that fishy odours – those characteristic smells that float around the house informing everyone that fish is definitely for dinner – are reduced to a minimum. These are sealed inside the pressure cooker until the last minute.

I hope you will enjoy trying the recipes that follow. Various types of fish are available today and most can be substituted for those given in the recipes. Try the less expensive coley to replace cod or haddock, for instance.

PRESSURE-COOKED FISH AND FREEZING

Fish overcooks so easily that it is not worth pressure-cooking it for the freezer. However, frozen fish can be cooked in the pressure cooker and may be substituted for fresh fish in the recipes which follow. No need to thaw it – just cook the fillets or fish pieces for the same time as its fresh counterpart. Thicker steaks and cutlets will probably need an extra minute added to the cooking time.

CHECKPOINTS FOR FISH

Fill the pressure cooker no more than half full with casserole-type recipes. The liquid must have space to boil up.

Use the trivet when the fish is to be cooked in steam rather in the liquid.

Remember to include at least the minimum amount of liquid (stock, water, wine, cider etc.) recommended by the manufacturer of your pressure cooker.

Cooking times depend on the type of fish and its preparation (whole, fillets, steaks). The table below gives cooking times.

Careful timing is especially important when pressure cooking fish as it is so easily overcooked. Reduce pressure with cold water where applicable, to speed up the process.

Clean, trim and wash the fish as you would for any other method of cooking. Remember to use less seasoning.

Thickening agents are best added after cooking unless a casserole is being prepared (when the fish is coated with a little flour before cooking).

To adapt your own fish recipes for pressure cooking, use the time chart below and the recipes as guides. The amount of liquid included will probably need to be reduced slightly too, but again look at the recipes for guidance.

The following times for pressure-cooking fish are for High/15-lb. pressure. If your pressure cooker is fixed at 7½-lb., simply double up on the times and follow the manufacturers' instructions on the amount of liquid to use.

White fish	*Cooking time at High/15-lb. pressure*
Bass, Bream, Brill, Cod, Coley, Haddock, Hake, Halibut, Ling, Plaice, Rock Salmon, Sole, Turbot	Steaks and fillets 3–6 minutes Whole fish 5–6 minutes per 1 lb/450 g.

Skate wings	3–6 minutes		
Whiting	Steaks and fillets		
	4–5 minutes		
	Whole fish 5–6 minutes per		
	1 lb./450 g.		

Oily fish			
Herring, Mackerel,	Whole fish 5–8 minutes		
Mullet, Trout			
Salmon	Steaks 6–8 minutes		
	Whole fish 6 minutes per		
	1 lb./450 g.		

Shellfish			
Crab	7–10 minutes		
Lobster	10 minutes		
Prawns, Shrimps	2–3 minutes		

Waitaki Fish Scallops

Serves 4

INGREDIENTS

	Imperial	Metric	American
Cod, Haddock or Hake fillets	1 lb.	450 g.	1 lb.
Medium onion	1	1	1
Bay leaf			
Parsley			
Salt	1 tsp.	1 tsp.	1 tsp.
Few peppercorns			
Malt vinegar	1 tsp.	1 tsp.	1 tsp.
Water	½ pt	300 ml.	1¼ cups
Sauce:			
Butter	3 tbsp.	3 tbsp.	3 tbsp.
Flour	1½ oz.	40 g.	⅓ cup
Milk	¼ pt	150 ml.	⅔ cup
Fish liquor	½ pt	300 ml.	1¼ cups
Cheese, grated	4 oz.	100 g.	¼ lb.
Lemon juice			
Salt and pepper			

Place the fish, whole onion, bay leaf, parsley, salt and peppercorns, vinegar and water in the pressure cooker (without the trivet). Bring to pressure and cook for given time. Reduce pressure. Lift out the fish, skin and flake it, then chop the onion. Strain the fish liquor. Wipe out the pressure cooker with kitchen paper.

To make the sauce, melt the butter in the open pressure cooker and in it sauté the chopped onion gently for a few minutes. Remove it from the heat and stir in the flour. When smooth, add the milk gradually and stir in ½ pt/300 ml./1¼ cups of the fish liquor (add water to make up the quantity if necessary). Cook gently for 3–5 minutes. Remove from the heat and stir in three-quarters of the cheese, seasoning to taste with lemon juice, salt and pepper. Thin it, if necessary, with a little more fish liquor.

Take four scallop shells or small ovenproof dishes and place a large spoonful of sauce on each. Divide the fish between the four shells, then cover the fish with the remaining sauce. Sprinkle it with the remaining grated cheese and brown under a hot grill. Just before serving, garnish with mustard and cress or watercress and lemon butterflies.

COOKING TIME
High/15-lb. pressure 4 minutes
Reduce pressure with cold water
Fixed 7½-lb. pressure 8 minutes

Devon Haddock

Serves 4

INGREDIENTS	Imperial	Metric	American
Haddock fillets, skinned and cut into cubes	4	4	4
Seasoned flour			
Butter	1 oz.	25 g.	2 tbsp.
Onions, chopped	2	2	2
Carrots, sliced	2	2	2
Green pepper, de-seeded and sliced	1	1	1
Cider	1 pt	500 ml.	2½ cups
Bay leaf			
Chopped parsley	1 tbsp.	1 tbsp.	1 tbsp.

Coat the haddock pieces with a little seasoned flour. Heat the butter in the open pressure cooker and in it sauté the vegetables lightly for 2–3 minutes. Stir in the haddock, then the cider. Add the bay leaf. Bring to pressure and cook for given time. Reduce pressure. Remove bay leaf and adjust seasoning if necessary. Stir in the chopped parsley just before serving.

COOKING TIME
High/15-lb. pressure 4 minutes
Reduce pressure with cold water
Fixed 7½-lb. pressure 8 minutes

Plaice Parcels

Serves 4

INGREDIENTS	Imperial	Metric	American
Butter	1 oz.	25 g.	2 tbsp.
Medium onion, chopped	1	1	1
Mushrooms, chopped	4 oz.	100 g.	$\frac{1}{4}$ lb.
Eggs, hard-boiled and chopped	2	2	2
Chopped parsley	2 tsp.	2 tsp.	2 tsp.
Salt and pepper			
Plaice fillets	8	8	8
Grated rind and juice	2 Oranges		
Bay leaf	1	1	1
Water			
Peppercorns	6	6	6
Cornflour/cornstarch	1–2 tbsp.	1–2 tbsp.	1–2 tbsp.

In a small frying pan heat the butter and in it sauté the onion and mushrooms gently for 3–4 minutes. Stir in the chopped egg and parsley and season to taste.

Season the plaice fillets and place a spoonful of the stuffing onto each. Roll up each fillet and secure it with a wooden cocktail stick. Arrange the fish in the pressure cooker (trivet removed). Make up the orange juice to $\frac{1}{2}$ pt/300 ml./1$\frac{1}{4}$ cups with water, season with a little salt and pepper and pour it round the fish. Add the orange rind, bay leaf and peppercorns. Bring to pressure and cook for given time. Reduce pressure. Arrange the plaice on a serving dish and keep it warm. Remove the bay leaf and peppercorns. Mix the cornflour with a little cold water to form a smooth paste and add it to the orange sauce. Bring to the boil, stirring well. Adjust the seasoning and pour the sauce over and around the plaice.

COOKING TIME
High/15-lb. pressure 4 minutes
Reduce pressure with cold water
Fixed 7$\frac{1}{2}$-lb. pressure 8 minutes

Piquant Plaice

Serves 4

INGREDIENTS	Imperial	Metric	American
Plaice fillets	1$\frac{1}{2}$ lb.	700 g.	1$\frac{1}{2}$ lb.
Salt and pepper			
Butter	1 oz.	25 g.	2 tbsp.
Small onion, chopped	1	1	1
Clove garlic, crushed	1	1	1
Tomato purée/paste	2 tbsp.	2 tbsp.	2 tbsp.
Worcestershire sauce	2 tsp.	2 tsp.	2 tsp.
Sugar	$\frac{1}{2}$ tsp.	$\frac{1}{2}$ tsp.	$\frac{1}{2}$ tsp.
Water	$\frac{1}{2}$ pt	300 ml.	1$\frac{1}{4}$ cups
Cornflour/cornstarch	1 tbsp.	1 tbsp.	1 tbsp.
Lemon wedges			

Skin the plaice fillets and season with salt and pepper. Roll them up and secure each with wooden cocktail sticks. Heat the butter in the open pressure cooker and in it sauté the onion and garlic gently till transparent. Add remaining ingredients, except the cornflour and lemon wedges, and stir well. Sit the plaice rolls in the sauce. Bring to pressure and cook for given time. Reduce pressure. Arrange the plaice rolls on a serving dish. Mix the cornflour with a little cold water to form a smooth paste and add it to the sauce. Bring to the boil, stirring well. Pour over and around the plaice and garnish with lemon wedges.

COOKING TIME
High/15-lb. pressure 4 minutes
Reduce pressure with cold water
Fixed 7$\frac{1}{2}$-lb. pressure 8 minutes

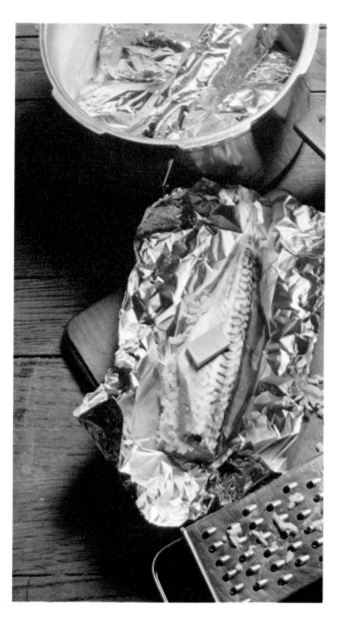

Stuffed Mackerel

 Serves 4

INGREDIENTS	Imperial	Metric	American
Mackerel, cleaned	4	4	4
Salt and pepper			
Eating apples, grated	2	2	2
Small onion, finely chopped	1	1	1
White breadcrumbs	2 oz.	50 g.	1 cup
Cheddar cheese, grated	4 oz.	100 g.	$\frac{1}{4}$ lb.
Butter, melted	2–3 oz.	50–75 g.	$\frac{1}{4}$–$\frac{1}{3}$ cup
Lemon twists			
Parsley			

Wipe the inside of the mackerel and season it inside and out with salt and pepper. Mix together the apple, onion, breadcrumbs and grated cheese. Season to taste, then bind the mixture with 2 tbsp. of the melted butter. Stuff the fish and secure it with wooden cocktail sticks. Place each fish on a separate sheet of foil. Pour the remaining melted butter over the mackerel. Fold the foil over and seal it to make four parcels.

Pour $\frac{1}{2}$ pt/300 ml./$1\frac{1}{4}$ cups water into the pressure cooker and position the trivet. Place the parcels on the trivet. Bring to pressure and cook for given time. Reduce pressure.

Open the parcels and arrange the mackerel on a warm serving dish. Pour any butter left in the foil over the fish and garnish them with lemon twists and parsley.

COOKING TIME
High/15-lb. pressure 6 minutes
Reduce pressure with cold water
Fixed 7$\frac{1}{2}$-lb. pressure 12 minutes

Note: Herring is also excellent cooked this way.

Smoked Haddock Casserole

 Serves 4

INGREDIENTS	Imperial	Metric	American
Butter	1 oz.	25 g.	2 tbsp.
Onions, chopped	2	2	2
Tomatoes, skinned and sliced	4	4	4
Frozen peas	4 oz.	100 g.	$\frac{1}{4}$ lb.
Smoked haddock, skinned, cut into cubes	1½ lb.	700 g.	1½ lb.
Pinch ground mace			
Sugar	2 tsp.	2 tsp.	2 tsp.
Salt and pepper			
Water	$\frac{3}{4}$ pt	400 ml.	2 cups
Flour	1 oz.	25 g.	$\frac{1}{4}$ cup
Milk	$\frac{1}{4}$ pt	150 ml.	$\frac{2}{3}$ cup
Chopped parsley			

Heat the butter in the open pressure cooker and in it sauté the onions till transparent. Stir in the tomatoes, frozen peas, smoked haddock, mace, sugar, seasoning and water. Bring to pressure and cook for given time. Reduce pressure.

Mix the flour with the milk to form a smooth paste and add it to the fish. Bring to the boil, stirring gently. Sprinkle with a little chopped parsley just before serving.

COOKING TIME
High/15-lb. pressure 3 minutes
Reduce pressure with cold water
Fixed 7½-lb. pressure 6 minutes

Haddock in Creole Sauce

 Serves 4

INGREDIENTS	Imperial	Metric	American
Cooking oil	2 tbsp.	2 tbsp.	2 tbsp.
Small onion, chopped	1	1	1
Clove garlic, crushed	1	1	1
Celery, chopped	1 stick	1 stick	1 stalk
Green pepper, de-seeded and chopped	1	1	1
Canned tomatoes	14 oz.	397 g.	1 lb.
Tomato purée or paste	1 tbsp.	1 tbsp.	1 tbsp.
Sugar	1 tsp.	1 tsp.	1 tsp.
Pinch basil			
Chilli powder	$\frac{1}{2}$ tsp.	$\frac{1}{2}$ tsp.	$\frac{1}{2}$ tsp.
Salt and pepper			
Haddock fillets, skinned and cut into cubes	4	4	4

Heat the oil in the open pressure cooker and in it sauté the onion, garlic, celery and pepper gently for 2–3 minutes. Stir in the tomatoes, including the juice made up to $\frac{1}{2}$ pt/300 ml./$1\frac{1}{4}$ cups with water. Add the tomato purée, sugar, basil, chilli powder, seasoning and haddock pieces. Bring to pressure and cook for given time. Reduce pressure.

COOKING TIME
High/15-lb. pressure 4 minutes
Reduce pressure with cold water
Fixed 7½-lb. pressure 8 minutes
Note: This recipe is equally good made with prawns. Replace the haddock with $\frac{1}{2}$ lb./225 g. peeled prawns and cook for 3 minutes at High/15-lb. pressure or 6 minutes at 7½-lb. pressure.

Cod Country Style

 Serves 4

INGREDIENTS	Imperial	Metric	American
Cod steaks	4	4	4
Salt and pepper			
Juice 1 lemon			
Butter	2 oz.	50 g.	$\frac{1}{4}$ cup
Clove garlic, crushed	1	1	1
Potatoes, thinly sliced	4	4	4
Onions, sliced	2	2	2
Canned tomatoes	14-oz.	397-g.	1 lb.
Water	$\frac{1}{4}$ pt	150 ml.	$\frac{2}{3}$ cup
Good pinch thyme			
Few sprigs parsley			

Place each cod steak on a separate piece of foil. Dot each with butter, season and sprinkle with lemon juice. Fold the foil over each steak and seal to form four parcels.

Heat the butter in the open pressure cooker and sauté the garlic, potatoes and onions for 2–3 minutes, seasoning well. Add the tomatoes, including the juice, water and thyme. Place the trivet on the vegetables then the cod parcels on top. Bring to pressure and cook for given time. Reduce pressure. Lift out the fish parcels and the trivet. Arrange the vegetables on a serving dish. Open the foil parcels and place the cod steaks on top of the vegetables. Pour any juice from the parcels over the steaks and garnish each with a sprig of parsley.

COOKING TIME
High/15-lb. pressure 5 minutes
Reduce pressure with cold water
Fixed 7½-lb. pressure 10 minutes

Soused Herrings

 Serves 4

INGREDIENTS	Imperial	Metric	American
Small herrings	8	8	8
Salt and pepper			
Dried red chilli	1	1	1
Blade mace	1	1	1
Bay leaf	1	1	1
Whole allspice	3	3	3
Black peppercorns	6	6	6
Small onions, thinly sliced	1–2	1–2	1–2
Malt vinegar	$\frac{1}{4}$ pt	150 ml.	$\frac{2}{3}$ cup
Water	$\frac{1}{4}$ pt	150 ml.	$\frac{2}{3}$ cup

Scale and clean the herrings, removing the heads and tails. Split and bone the fish. Lightly season the fillets on the fleshy side with salt and pepper. Roll each up from the tail end, skin side outside, and secure each roll with a wooden cocktail stick. Place the herrings in the pressure cooker (without the trivet) and add the remaining ingredients. Bring to pressure and cook for given time. Reduce pressure.

Arrange the herrings in a serving dish and pour the liquor over the fish. Allow it to cool and serve as a starter or with a salad and boiled potatoes as a main dish.

COOKING TIME
High/15-lb. pressure 6 minutes
Reduce pressure with cold water
Fixed 7$\frac{1}{2}$-lb. pressure 10 minutes

Note: Boned mackerel or pilchards may also be prepared in this way.

Tuna Fish

Serves 4

INGREDIENTS	Imperial	Metric	American
Canned tuna fish	7-oz.	198-g.	$\frac{1}{2}$ lb.
Lemon juice	2 tsp.	2 tsp.	2 tsp.
Pinch dried basil			
Cooking oil	2 tbsp.	2 tbsp.	2 tbsp.
Onions, chopped	2	2	2
Mushrooms, sliced	4 oz.	100 g.	$\frac{1}{4}$ lb.
Canned tomatoes	14-oz.	397-g.	1 lb.
Water	$\frac{1}{4}$ pt	150 ml.	$\frac{2}{3}$ cup
Sherry (optional)	2 tbsp.	2 tbsp.	2 tbsp.
Mustard	2 tsp.	2 tsp.	2 tsp.
Salt and pepper			

Sprinkle the tuna with the lemon juice and basil, then flake the fish with a fork. Heat the oil in the open pressure cooker and in it sauté the onions till transparent. Stir in the remaining ingredients, bring to pressure and cook for given time. Reduce pressure.

If liked, thicken the sauce with a little flour mixed with cold water. Serve with buttered noodles or spaghetti.

COOKING TIME
High/15-lb. pressure 5 minutes
Reduce pressure with cold water
Fixed 7$\frac{1}{2}$-lb. pressure 10 minutes

Apple Sole

 Serves 4

INGREDIENTS

	Imperial	Metric	American
Fillets sole	6	6	6
Salt and pepper			
Apple juice	$\frac{1}{2}$ pt	300 ml.	$1\frac{1}{4}$ cups
Cornflour or Cornstarch	2 tsp.	2 tsp.	2 tsp.
Single or thin cream	$\frac{1}{4}$ pt	150 ml.	$\frac{2}{3}$ cup
Chopped parsley			

Season the sole fillets and roll them up, skin side inside. Arrange the rolls in the pressure cooker (without the trivet) and pour the apple juice around them. Bring to pressure and cook for given time. Reduce pressure.

Lift the fish rolls on to a warm serving dish. Mix the cornflour with a little cold water to form a smooth paste and add it to the apple juice. Bring to the boil, stirring well. Stir in the cream, reheat the sauce gently and pour it over the fish. Sprinkle with a little chopped parsley and serve.

COOKING TIME
High/15-lb. pressure 4 minutes
Reduce pressure with cold water
Fixed $7\frac{1}{2}$-lb. pressure 8 minutes

CHECKPOINT
Do not boil the sauce when reheating or the cream will separate.

VEGETABLES

Great savings in both time and fuel are made when pressure-cooking vegetables, particularly if several are prepared together.

As the minimum amount of water is used and the vegetables are cooked in steam, colour, flavour, texture and food value are retained too. However, make sure that nothing is wasted by using the cooking liquor in a tasty sauce or gravy.

My pressure cooker helps me to make full use of dried vegetables. Many of these provide rich and tasty sources of protein, but are often left out of the diet because they need lengthy preparation. When pressure cooking, there is no need to soak dried vegetables overnight. Just cover them with boiling water, leave for one hour, then use.

The pressure cooker can also be used for blanching vegetables for the freezer, without the need for masses of water (and therefore steam). A blanching basket is offered with some pressure cookers, and this makes the process even simpler. Timing is crucial though so use an automatic timer and follow the instructions opposite.

VEGETABLES AND FREEZING

Generally, it is not worth pressure-cooking vegetables for the freezer, except as purées for use in soups.

Frozen vegetables *should not* be thawed before pressure cooking. Just cook them the same time as you would the fresh vegetable. Most frozen vegetables cook so quickly anyway that you may not feel it is worth using the pressure cooker.

BLANCHING

Vegetables are blanched by bringing to Medium/10-lb. pressure for a specific time. Your instruction book will give details of vegetable blanching in your particular model, so check first to see that it can be done. Here, though, are some general rules.

Prepare the vegetables according to kind.

Pour $\frac{1}{2}$ pt/300 ml./$1\frac{1}{4}$ cups boiling water into the pressure cooker and position the trivet. Add the vegetables, using the perforated separators for small and green vegetables. Other vegetables can be place on the trivet. The pressure cooker should not be more than two-thirds full – space must be left for the steam to circulate.

Bring to Medium/10-lb. pressure for the given time (refer to chart).

Reduce pressure quickly with cold water, take off the lid and plunge the vegetables immediately into cold water.

Drain and dry the vegetables then pack, seal and label them for freezing.

CHECKPOINTS FOR FRESH VEGETABLES

The pressure cooker should not be more than two-thirds full of vegetables, to allow space for the steam to circulate.

The trivet is used when the vegetables are to be cooked in steam. Separators keep the vegetables apart and enable easy removal from the pressure cooker when hot.

Check the manufacturers' instruction for the minimum amount of liquid needed during cooking.

Cooking times will depend on the type, age, freshness and size of the vegetables. Accuracy is important if vegetables are not to overcook. The chart opposite gives cooking times.

When pressure-cooking more than one vegetable at one time, check their cooking times. Vegetables needing longer cooking may need to be cut smaller. With practice you will be able to cook several vegetables to their correct degree of doneness. Should a vegetable not be cooked in the time, it is a simple matter to bring the pressure cooker back to pressure for an extra minute. Most root vegetables will take the same time to cook if cut into equal-sized pieces.

Do not be too heavy-handed with seasoning

when pressure-cooking vegetables, since they retain so much of their own mineral salts. Remember too that when boiling vegetables in an ordinary saucepan much salt is let out into the cooking water. This does not happen in the pressure cooker.

Use the cooking liquor in a sauce or a gravy, or as a basis for a soup or casserole.

The following times for pressure-cooking fresh vegetables are for High/15-lb. pressure. If your pressure cooker is fixed at 7½-lb., just double the times given below and follow the manufacturers' instructions on the amount of liquid to use. Blanching times are for Medium/10-lb. pressure only.

Vegetable	Cooking time High/15-lb. pressure	Blanching time Medium/10-lb. pressure
Artichokes, Globe	6–10 minutes depending on size	3–5 minutes depending on size
Jerusalem	4–6 minutes	
Asparagus, bundles	2–4 minutes	bring to pressure only
Beans, Broad	3–5 minutes	1 minute
French	3 minutes	bring to pressure only
Runner	4 minutes	bring to pressure only
Beetroot, small	10 minutes	7 minutes, sliced
medium	15–20 minutes	
large	20–30 minutes	
Broccoli spears	3–4 minutes	1 minute
Brussels Sprouts	3–4 minutes	1 minute
Cabbage, shredded	3 minutes	bring to pressure only
Carrots, sliced	3–4 minutes	2 minutes
Cauliflower, florets	3–4 minutes	1 minute
whole	5–8 minutes	
Celery, short sticks	3 minutes	2 minutes
Celeriac, cubes	3 minutes	1 minute
Chicory, whole	3–6 minutes	
Corn on the cob	3–5 minutes depending on size	2–3 minutes depending on size
Courgettes, sliced	3 minutes	bring to pressure only
Fennel, halves	3–6 minutes	1 minute
Leeks, sliced	3–4 minutes	1 minute
Marrow, thick slices	3–4 minutes	2 minutes
Onions, whole	6–8 minutes	
sliced	3–4 minutes	
Parsnips, sliced	3–4 minutes	1 minute
Peas	3–4 minutes	1 minute
Potatoes, new whole	4–5 minutes	2 minutes
old quarters	3–4 minutes	
Spinach	1–2 minutes	bring to pressure only
Swede, cubes	4 minutes	1 minute
Turnip, sliced or small whole	3–4 minutes	2 minutes

DRIED VEGETABLES

Dried vegetables do not need overnight soaking. Put the vegetables into a large basin and cover them with plenty of boiling water. Put a plate over the bowl and leave the beans to soak for one hour.

Pour into the pressure cooker 1¾ pt/1 l./4½ cups liquid for every 1 lb./450 g. vegetables. Make up the soaking water from the vegetables to the required amount with more water.

Bring to the boil and add the vegetables. The pressure cooker should not be more than half full. Season to taste and bring it back to the boil.

Skim the surface of the liquid, then lower the heat till the contents boil gently. Bring to pressure on this heat and cook for the given time.

Always reduce pressure slowly.

Dried vegetable	Cooking time	
	High/15-lb. pressure	7½-lb. pressure
Butter beans	20 minutes	40 minutes
Haricot beans, small	20 minutes	40 minutes
large	30 minutes	1 hour
Lentils	15 minutes	30 minutes
Peas, whole	20 minutes	40 minutes
split	15 minutes	30 minutes

Note: Split varieties, such as lentils or peas, may be added to soups, casseroles etc., without pre-soaking.

Ratatouille

 Serves 4–6

INGREDIENTS

	Imperial	Metric	American
Cooking oil	4 tbsp.	4 tbsp.	4 tbsp.
Onions, chopped	2	2	2
Cloves garlic, crushed	1–2	1–2	1–2
Green peppers, de-seeded and sliced	2	2	2
Tomatoes, skinned and sliced	1 lb.	450 g.	1 lb.
Large aubergine, sliced	1	1	1
Courgettes, sliced	4	4	4
Water	¼ pt	150 ml.	⅔ cup
(If 7½-lb. pressure)	½ pt	300 ml.	1¼ cups
Tomato purée or paste	2 tbsp.	2 tbsp.	2 tbsp.
Salt and pepper			

Heat the oil in the open pressure cooker and in it sauté the onions and garlic till transparent. Stir in the remaining ingredients, bring to pressure and cook for given time. Reduce pressure.

COOKING TIME
High/15-lb. pressure 5 minutes
Reduce pressure with cold water
Fixed 7½-lb. pressure 10 minutes

TO FREEZE
Pack in rigid polythene container, cover and freeze. Thaw at room temperature and reheat gently.

Stuffed Peppers

 Serves 4

INGREDIENTS

	Imperial	Metric	American
Medium green peppers	4	4	4
Cooked chicken, chopped	8 oz.	225 g.	$\frac{1}{2}$ lb.
Small onions, chopped	2	2	2
Streaky bacon or bacon slices, chopped	4 oz.	100 g.	$\frac{1}{4}$ lb.
Cooked long-grain rice	12 oz.	350 g.	$\frac{3}{4}$ lb.
Dried ground cumin	1 tsp.	1 tsp.	1 tsp.
Salt and pepper			

Cut off the stem end of the peppers and scoop out the seeds. Mix together the remaining ingredients, seasoning well. Fill each pepper with equal portions of the stuffing mixture. Pour $\frac{1}{2}$ pt/300 ml./$1\frac{1}{4}$ cups water into the pressure cooker and position the trivet. Stand the stuffed peppers on the trivet, bring to pressure and cook for given time. Reduce pressure. Lift the peppers on to a serving dish and garnish them with a few crispy-grilled pieces of bacon.

COOKING TIME
High/15-lb. pressure 4 minutes
Reduce pressure with cold water
Fixed 7$\frac{1}{2}$-lb. pressure 8 minutes
Note: When reducing pressure, take care not to tilt the pressure cooker, causing the peppers to topple and the stuffing to spill out.

Stuffed Cabbage

Serves 6

INGREDIENTS

	Imperial	Metric	American
Butter	1 oz.	25 g.	2 tbsp.
Minced beef/Hamburger	1 lb.	450 g.	1 lb.
Small onion, chopped	1	1	1
Clove garlic, crushed	1	1	1
Cooked long-grain rice	1 oz.	25 g.	2–3 tbsp.
Good pinch mixed herbs			
Good pinch mixed spice			
Salt and pepper			
Large cabbage leaves	12	12	12
Beef stock	$\frac{1}{2}$ pt	300 ml.	$1\frac{1}{4}$ cups
(If 7$\frac{1}{2}$-lb. pressure)	$\frac{3}{4}$ pt	400 ml.	2 cups
Canned condensed tomato soup	10$\frac{1}{2}$-oz.	298-g.	medium

Heat the butter in a frying pan and in it brown the minced beef for 4–5 minutes. Stir in the onion and garlic and cook gently for a further few minutes. Stir in the rice, herbs, spice and seasoning.

Blanch the cabbage leaves by putting them in boiling water for 2 minutes. Dry well with kitchen paper. Place some filling in the centre of each leaf and roll the leaf up, tucking in the ends to form neat parcels. Arrange the cabbage rolls in the pressure cooker (without the trivet) and pour the beef stock around the rolls. Bring to pressure and cook for given time. Reduce pressure. Lift the cabbage on to a warm serving dish. Carefully stir the condensed soup into the stock and reheat. Pour some sauce over and around the cabbage and serve the rest separately.

COOKING TIME
High/15-lb. pressure 15 minutes
Reduce pressure with cold water
Fixed 7$\frac{1}{2}$-lb. pressure 25 minutes

Spiced Cabbage

 Serves 4

INGREDIENTS

	Imperial	Metric	American
Butter	2 oz.	50 g.	$\frac{1}{4}$ cup
Small onion, chopped	1	1	1
Small red cabbage, shredded	1	1	1
Cooking apple, peeled, cored, chopped	1	1	1
Sultanas	1 oz.	25 g.	2 tbsp.
Wine vinegar	2 tbsp.	2 tbsp.	2 tbsp.
Water	2 tbsp.	2 tbsp.	2 tbsp.
(If 7$\frac{1}{2}$ lb. pressure)	4 tbsp.	4 tbsp.	4 tbsp.
Brown sugar	1 tbsp.	1 tbsp.	1 tbsp.
Salt and pepper			

Heat the butter in the open pressure cooker and in it sauté the onion gently till transparent. Add the remaining ingredients, bring to pressure and cook for given time. Reduce pressure. Serve hot or cold with cold cooked meat.

COOKING TIME
High/15-lb. pressure 4 minutes
Reduce pressure with cold water
Fixed 7$\frac{1}{2}$-lb. pressure 8 minutes

TO FREEZE
Pack into rigid polythene container, cover and freeze. Thaw at room temperature.

Note: This recipe probably does not include the minimum amount of liquid recommended by the manufacturer of your pressure cooker. It may, however, be successfully prepared where $\frac{1}{4}$–$\frac{1}{2}$ pt/150–300 ml./$\frac{2}{3}$–1$\frac{1}{2}$ cups liquid is required.

Celery in Tomato Sauce

 Serves 4

INGREDIENTS	Imperial	Metric	American
Butter	1 oz.	25 g.	2 tbsp.
Clove garlic, crushed	1	1	1
Large head celery, cut into stalks	1	1	1
Canned tomatoes	8-oz.	226-g.	$\frac{1}{2}$ lb.
Pinch mixed herbs			
Chicken stock	$\frac{1}{4}$ pt	150 ml.	$\frac{2}{3}$ cup
Flour	1–2 tbsp.	1–2 tbsp.	1–2 tbsp.

Heat the butter in the open pressure cooker and in it sauté the garlic and celery gently for 1–2 minutes. Pour the tomatoes and their juices over the celery and add the mixed herbs, chicken stock and seasoning. Stir well, bring to pressure and cook for given time. Reduce pressure.

Mix the flour with a little cold water to form a smooth paste and stir it into the sauce. Bring to the boil, stirring continuously.

COOKING TIME
High/15-lb. pressure 4 minutes
Reduce pressure with cold water
Fixed 7$\frac{1}{2}$-lb. pressure 8 minutes

Potato Pie

 Serves 4

INGREDIENTS	Imperial	Metric	American
Butter			
Potatoes, peeled and sliced thinly	1$\frac{1}{2}$ lb.	700 g.	1$\frac{1}{2}$ lb.
Onions, chopped	2	2	2
Ground nutmeg			
Salt and pepper			
Chicken stock	$\frac{1}{4}$ pt	150 ml.	$\frac{2}{3}$ cup
Cheese, grated	2 oz.	50 g.	$\frac{1}{4}$ cup

Butter an ovenproof dish which will fit into the pressure cooker. Layer the potatoes and onions in the dish. Sprinkle each layer with a little ground nutmeg and season well with salt and pepper. Pour chicken stock over the potatoes.

Pour $\frac{1}{2}$ pt/300 ml./1$\frac{1}{4}$ cups water into pressure cooker (1 pt/500 ml./2$\frac{1}{4}$ cups for fixed 7$\frac{1}{2}$-lb. pressure) and place the trivet in position. Stand the dish on the trivet, bring to pressure and cook for given time. Reduce pressure. Sprinkle the cheese over the potatoes and brown them under the grill before serving.

COOKING TIME
High/15-lb. pressure 13 minutes
Reduce pressure with cold water
Fixed 7$\frac{1}{2}$-lb. pressure 25 minutes

Note: New potatoes might need slightly longer cooking times than those given.

This dish is also delicious made with garlic (omitting the nutmeg) and using canned tomatoes instead of the chicken stock.

Spicy Stuffed Onions

Serves 4

INGREDIENTS

	Imperial	Metric	American
Large onions	4	4	4
Breadcrumbs	4 oz.	100 g.	2 cups
Chopped mushrooms	4 tbsp.	4 tbsp.	4 tbsp.
Chutney	2 tbsp.	2 tbsp.	2 tbsp.
Curry powder	3 tsp.	3 tsp.	3 tsp.
Worcestershire sauce	4 tsp.	4 tsp.	4 tsp.
Salt			
Freshly-ground black pepper			

Using a teaspoon, scoop the centre out of each onion. Take a thin slice off the base of each with a sharp knife, so they will stand. In a bowl, mix together the remaining ingredients. Stuff each onion with the mixture. Pour $\frac{1}{2}$ pt/300 ml./$1\frac{1}{4}$ cups water into the pressure cooker and position the trivet. Stand the onions on the trivet. Bring to pressure and cook for given time. Reduce pressure. Garnish the onions with sprigs of parsley and serve.

COOKING TIME

High/15-lb. pressure 8 minutes
Reduce pressure with cold water
Fixed 7$\frac{1}{2}$-lb. pressure 16 minutes

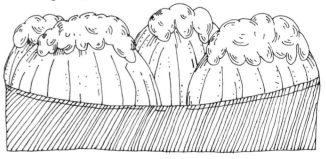

Savoury Stuffed Tomatoes

Serves 4

INGREDIENTS	Imperial	Metric	American
Large tomatoes	4	4	4
Butter	$\frac{1}{2}$ oz.	15 g.	1 tbsp.
Rasher bacon, chopped	1	1	1
Small onion, chopped	1	1	1
White breadcrumbs	$1\frac{1}{2}$ oz.	40 g.	$\frac{3}{4}$ cup
Chopped parsley	1 tsp.	1 tsp.	1 tsp.
Pinch sage			
Salt and pepper			

Cut the tops off the tomatoes and remove the pulp. Heat the butter in a small frying pan and in it sauté the bacon and onion gently for 2–3 minutes. Add half of the chopped tomato pulp and the breadcrumbs, parsley, sage and seasoning. Stuff the tomatoes with this mixture and replace their tops. Pour $\frac{1}{2}$ pt/300 ml./$1\frac{1}{4}$ cups water into the pressure cooker and position the trivet. Stand the tomatoes on top. Bring to pressure and cook for given time. Reduce pressure.

COOKING TIME
High/15-lb. pressure 2 minutes
Reduce pressure with cold water
Fixed $7\frac{1}{2}$-lb. pressure 4 minutes

Note: When reducing pressure, take care not to tilt the pressure cooker, causing the tomatoes inside to topple.

Cauliflower Niçoise

 Serves 4

INGREDIENTS	Imperial	Metric	American
Cooking oil	1 tbsp.	1 tbsp.	1 tbsp.
Butter	1 oz.	25 g.	2 tbsp.
Onion, chopped	1	1	1
Clove garlic, crushed	1	1	1
Cauliflower, cut into florets	1	1	1
Canned tomatoes	14-oz.	397-g.	1 lb.
Chicken stock	$\frac{1}{4}$ pt	150 ml.	$\frac{2}{3}$ cup
(If 7$\frac{1}{2}$-lb. pressure)	$\frac{1}{2}$ pt	300 ml.	1$\frac{1}{4}$ cups
Dried basil	$\frac{1}{2}$–1 tsp.	$\frac{1}{2}$–1 tsp.	$\frac{1}{2}$–1 tsp.
Salt and pepper			
Black olives, stoned	6–8	6–8	6–8

Heat the oil and butter in the open pressure cooker and in it sauté the onion and garlic till transparent. Stir in the remaining ingredients, bring to pressure and cook for given time. Reduce pressure.

COOKING TIME
High/15-lb. pressure 5 minutes
Reduce pressure with cold water
Fixed 7$\frac{1}{2}$-lb. pressure 10 minutes

Onion Butter Beans

 Serves 4

INGREDIENTS	Imperial	Metric	American
Dried butter beans	8 oz.	225 g.	$\frac{1}{2}$ lb.
Butter	2 oz.	50 g.	$\frac{1}{4}$ cup
Large onions, chopped	2	2	2
Good pinch mace			
Salt and pepper			
Water			
Milk	$\frac{1}{4}$ pt	150 ml.	$\frac{2}{3}$ cup
Flour	3–4 tbsp.	3–4 tbsp.	3–4 tbsp.
Cheese, grated	4 oz.	100 g.	$\frac{1}{4}$ lb.

Place the butter beans in a dish and cover with boiling water. Leave to soak for one hour. Heat the butter in the open pressure cooker and gently sauté the onions in it till transparent. Add the drained butter beans, mace and seasoning. Make the soaking liquid from the beans up to 1 pt/550 ml./2$\frac{1}{4}$ cups with water (1$\frac{1}{4}$ pt/700 ml./3 cups if fixed 7$\frac{1}{2}$-lb. pressure) and stir into the bean mixture. Bring to pressure and cook for given time. Reduce pressure.

Mix the flour with a little of the milk to form a smooth paste and add it to the beans. Stir in the rest of the milk. Bring to the boil, stirring well. Pour the beans into an ovenproof serving dish and sprinkle them with the grated cheese. Brown under a hot grill before serving.

COOKING TIME
High/15-lb. pressure 20 minutes
Reduce pressure slowly
Fixed 7$\frac{1}{2}$-lb. pressure 40 minutes

DESSERTS

Fruits (fresh or dried), custards, milk puddings and sponge puddings are all ideal candidates for pressure-cooking. Enormous time and fuel savings are involved when pressure-cooking most desserts.

Fresh fruits can be quickly cooked or puréed in your pressure cooker – a great advantage to freezer owners, particularly during the soft fruit season.

Dried fruits need only a few minutes soaking in boiling water before pressure-cooking and can therefore be used to make speedy desserts.

Unexpectedly, perhaps, egg custards cook perfectly in your pressure cooker without the usual temperature watching. An automatic timer is a 'must' though.

A big advantage when pressure-cooking steamed puddings is the lack of steam. In addition, there is no need for constant checking to see if there is sufficient water in the pan.

DESSERTS AND FREEZING

Sponge and suet puddings are best frozen uncooked and should be thawed before pressure-cooking. Left over sponge pudding may be frozen and then reheated at High/15-lb. pressure for 3–5 minutes, or fixed 7½-lb. pressure for 6–10 minutes.

Pressure-cooked fruits freeze well, particularly as purées, to be used when convenient for tarts, crumbles etc., or simply served as they are with cream. To freeze, pack them into polythene containers, cover and freeze. Fruits may also be softened and frozen during the season, ready for jam-making at a more convenient time.

Egg custards and milk puddings are not suitable for freezing, but egg custards may be frozen in the raw state.

CHECKPOINTS FOR FRESH FRUITS

The pressure cooker should not be more than half full when cooking fresh fruit.

Cooking times will depend on the type of fruit, its preparation (whole, halved, sliced etc.) and its degree of ripeness. The table below gives approximate cooking times.

Pour at least the minimum amount of liquid into the pressure cooker. This is usually ½ pt/300 ml./1¼ cups, but check with your instruction book.

Fruits are easier to handle if cooked in an ovenproof container or a solid separator supplied with the pressure cooker. Just layer the fruit, sprinkling it with caster sugar, and pour some water or sugar syrup (made with 3–4 tbsp. sugar and ¼ pt/150 ml./⅔ cup water) over it. Cover the container and stand it on the trivet for pressure cooking. Remember to include sufficient water beneath the trivet.

When making purées or cooking hard fruits, such as pears, the fruit may be placed straight into the pressure cooker (without the trivet) with the correct amount of water or syrup.

Reduce pressure with cold water when possible

Fruit	Cooking time at	
	High/15-lb. pressure	7½-lb. pressure
Apricots, Cherries, Damsons, Greengages (halved)	Bring to pressure	1 minute only
Pears, Peaches (halved)	3–5 minutes	10 minutes
Hard pears	8–10 minutes	15–20 minutes

	Medium/10-lb. pressure	7½ lb. pressure
Black currants, Gooseberries, Loganberries, Raspberries, Plums, Rhubarb	Bring to pressure only on medium heat	1 minute
Apple (slices)	1 minute	2 minutes

TO PRESSURE-COOK DRIED FRUITS

Place the fruit in a bowl and cover it with boiling water. Pour over 1 pt/550 ml./2½ cups for every 1 lb./450 g. dried fruit. Cover with a plate and leave to stand for 10 minutes.

Place the fruit and soaking liquid in the pressure cooker (without the trivet) and add sugar and flavourings (such as lemon or orange rind and juice, cloves, spices) to taste.

Do not fill the pressure cooker more than half full, as the fruit will expand during cooking.

Bring to pressure and cook for given time (see table below). Reduce pressure slowly.

Fruit	Cooking time at	
	High/15-lb. pressure	7½-lb. pressure
Apples	6 minutes	12 minutes
Apricots	3 minutes	5 minutes
Figs, Pears, Prunes, Mixed Fruit	10 minutes	20 minutes
Peaches	5 minutes	10 minutes

STEAMED PUDDINGS

An ovenproof container should be used for puddings. Make sure it fits easily into the pressure cooker. When using ovenproof glass or china, it is advisable to add 5–10 minutes to the cooking time.

The container should not be more than two-thirds full – the pudding must have space to rise. It is a good idea, when covering the pudding, to make a pleat in the foil or greaseproof paper in case the pudding rises above the rim. Always secure the foil or greaseproof paper firmly on to the container, preferably with string.

Refer to your manufacturers' instructions about the amount of water to include for steaming. The quantity will depend on the cooking time but should not be less than 1½ pt/1 l./4 cups.

A little vinegar in the water will prevent discoloration of the pressure cooker where hard water is used.

Take care not to allow the water to boil while preparing the pudding or you may not have sufficient water left for cooking. For the same reason it is a good idea to put boiling water into the pressure cooker rather than to bring cold water to the boil.

The trivet is used as a stand for the pudding.

Puddings are usually pre-steamed before pressure cooking. This helps to produce a light texture in the finished pudding. The lid is fitted on and the pressure cooker placed on a low heat (*without* the pressure weight or rotating valve) so that the water simmers and steam escapes gently from the vent. At the end of the pre-steaming period, the pressure weight or rotating valve is placed in position and the pressure cooker is brought to pressure for the required time.

Pressure should be reduced slowly.

When converting your own recipes for pressure-cooking the following guide may be useful:

Normal steaming time	Pre-steaming time	Pressure-cooking time	
		Low/5-lb.	7½ lb.
30 minutes	5 minutes	10 minutes	8 minutes
1 hour	15 minutes	25 minutes	20 minutes
2–3 hours	20 minutes	50–60 minutes	40–45 minutes

Date Pudding

Serves 4

INGREDIENTS	Imperial	Metric	American
Self-raising flour or flour sifted with 1 tsp. baking powder	4 oz.	100 g.	1 cup
Mixed spice	½ tsp.	½ tsp.	½ tsp.
Pinch salt			
Butter	3 oz.	75 g.	⅓ cup
Rounded tbsp. breadcrumbs	4	4	4
Rounded tbsp. brown sugar	2	2	2
Dates, chopped	4 oz.	100 g.	¼ lb.
Eggs, beaten	2	2	2
Golden syrup	1 tbsp.	1 tbsp.	1 tbsp.
Milk to mix			

Butter a 1½-pt/1-l./4-cup pudding basin.

Sieve together the flour, spice and salt. Rub in the butter then stir in the breadcrumbs, sugar and chopped dates. Mix together the eggs and syrup and add them to the dry ingredients. Mix well, adding a little milk if necessary to make a smooth dropping consistency. Put the mixture into the prepared basin and cover securely with foil or a double layer of greaseproof paper.

Pour 1½ pt/1 l./4 cups water into the pressure cooker and position the trivet. Stand the pudding on the trivet. Pre-steam the pudding (see page 83), then bring to pressure and cook for given time. Reduce pressure. Serve with custard.

COOKING TIME
Pre-steaming 25 minutes
Low/5-lb. pressure 25 minutes
Reduce pressure slowly
Fixed 7½-lb. pressure 20 minutes

Apricot Condé

Serves 4

INGREDIENTS	Imperial	Metric	American
Quantity Vanilla Rice Pudding	See page 87		
Single or thin cream	2 tbsp.	2 tbsp.	2 tbsp.
Cooked dried apricots			

Cook the rice pudding as indicated in the recipe and allow it to cool. Mix the cold rice pudding with a little cream and some drained chopped apricots. Spoon it into individual dishes and decorate with more fruit.

Note: This may be served with cooked fresh fruit or canned fruit.

Peaches in Vanilla Sauce

 Serves 4

INGREDIENTS

	Imperial	Metric	American
Medium peaches	4	4	4
Sugar	1 oz.	25 g.	2 tbsp.
Vanilla essence	1 tsp.	1 tsp.	1 tsp.
Water	$\frac{1}{4}$ pt	150 ml.	$\frac{2}{3}$ cup
Dry cider or white wine	$\frac{1}{4}$ pt	150 ml.	$\frac{2}{3}$ cup
Cornflour or Cornstarch	1 tbsp.	1 tbsp.	1 tbsp.
Single or thin cream	$\frac{1}{4}$ pt	150 ml.	$\frac{2}{3}$ cup

Skin the peaches by plunging them into boiling water for 1–2 minutes. Halve and stone them. Arrange the peaches in the pressure cooker (without the trivet) and sprinkle them with the sugar. Add vanilla essence, water and cider or wine. Bring to pressure and cook for given time. Reduce pressure.

Arrange the peach halves on a serving dish. Mix the cornflour with a little cold water to form a smooth paste and add it to the liquor in the pressure cooker. Bring to the boil, stirring well. Just before serving, stir the cream into the hot (not boiling) sauce and pour it over the peaches.

COOKING TIME
High/15-lb. pressure 4 minutes
Reduce pressure with cold water
Fixed $7\frac{1}{2}$-lb. pressure 8 minutes

Crème Caramel

Serves 4

INGREDIENTS	Imperial	Metric	American
Caramel:			
Water	$\frac{1}{4}$ pt	150 ml.	$\frac{2}{3}$ cup
Sugar	4 oz.	100 g.	$\frac{1}{2}$ cup
Custard:			
Eggs, beaten	3	3	3
Sugar	1 oz.	25 g.	2 tbsp.
Few drops vanilla essence			
Milk	$\frac{3}{4}$ pt	400 ml.	2 cups

To make the caramel: put the sugar and water into a small saucepan and dissolve the sugar slowly over a low heat. Bring to the boil, until it caramelizes (turns a golden brown). Pour the caramel into four warmed cups or bowls. Allow it to cool.

Mix together the eggs, sugar and vanilla essence. Warm the milk and pour it on to the eggs. Strain this mixture and pour it over the cooled caramel. Cover the cups or bowls securely with foil or a double layer of greaseproof paper.

Pour $\frac{1}{2}$ pt/300 ml./$1\frac{1}{4}$ cups water into the pressure cooker, position the trivet and stand the cups or bowls on top.

Bring to pressure and cook for given time. Reduce pressure. Chill for several hours before serving. To serve, ease the edge of the custard away from the dish and turn it out.

COOKING TIME

High/15-lb. pressure 3 minutes
Reduce pressure slowly
Fixed $7\frac{1}{2}$-lb. pressure 5 minutes
Note: The shape and size of the dishes used will determine exact cooking times. You will probably need to experiment with your own dishes to find the correct time. Crème Caramel is easier to turn out if really cold.

Egg Custard

Serves 4

INGREDIENTS	Imperial	Metric	American
Eggs, beaten	3	3	3
Caster or Superfine sugar	2 oz.	50 g.	$\frac{1}{4}$ cup
Few drops almond essence			
Milk	1 pt	550 ml.	$2\frac{1}{2}$ cups
Grated nutmeg			

Mix together the eggs, sugar and almond essence. Warm the milk and blend with the eggs. Pour the mixture into a buttered $1\frac{1}{2}$-pt/1-l./4-cup basin. Sprinkle with a little grated nutmeg and cover securely with foil or a double layer of greaseproof paper.

Pour 1 pt/500 ml./$2\frac{1}{2}$ cups water into the pressure cooker. Position the trivet and stand the basin on top. Bring to pressure and cook for given time. Reduce pressure.

COOKING TIME

High·15-lb. pressure 10 minutes
Reduce pressure slowly
Fixed $7\frac{1}{2}$-lb. pressure 20 minutes
Note: Other flavourings may be used to replace the almond essence. Try vanilla essence or a few teaspoons of instant coffee, dissolved in a little cold water.

Vanilla Rice Pudding

 Serves 4

INGREDIENTS

	Imperial	Metric	American
Butter	*1 oz.*	*25 g.*	*2 tbsp.*
Milk	*1 pt*	*550 ml.*	*2½ cups*
Pudding rice	*2 oz.*	*50 g.*	*⅓ cup*
Sugar	*2 oz.*	*50 g.*	*¼ cup*
Vanilla essence	*1 tsp.*	*1 tsp.*	*1 tsp.*
Good pinch grated nutmeg			

Melt the butter in the open pressure cooker (without the trivet) and pour in the milk. Bring to the boil and add the remaining ingredients. Bring to the boil again, then lower the heat so that the milk simmers gently. Bring to pressure on this heat and cook for given time. Reduce pressure.

Stir the pudding and pour it into a warm serving dish. If liked, brown it under a hot grill before serving.

COOKING TIME

High/15-lb. pressure 12 minutes
Reduce pressure slowly
Fixed 7½-lb. pressure 20 minutes
Reduce pressure slowly (without lifting rotating valve).

Note: Try using cinnamon or mixed spice to replace the vanilla and nutmeg.

Banana and Prune Bake

Serves 4

INGREDIENTS

	Imperial	Metric	American
Dried prunes	*8 oz.*	*225 g.*	*½ lb.*
Sugar	*2 oz.*	*50 g.*	*¼ cup*
Concentrated orange juice	*6 fl. oz.*	*175 ml.*	*⅔ cup*
Arrowroot	*2 tbsp.*	*2 tbsp.*	*2 tbsp.*
Bananas	*2*	*2*	*2*
Juice 1 lemon			
Butter	*1 oz.*	*25 g.*	*2 tbsp.*

Place the prunes in a bowl and cover them with boiling water. Cover with a plate and leave for 1 hour. Drain the prunes, reserving the liquid, arrange them in the pressure cooker (without the trivet) and sprinkle them with sugar. Make up the soaking liquid from the prunes to ½ pt/300 ml./1¼ cups with water and mix with the concentrated orange juice. Add the orange mixture to the prunes, bring to pressure and cook for given time. Reduce pressure.

Using a draining spoon lift out the prunes and arrange them in four small ovenproof dishes. Mix the arrowroot with a little cold water to form a smooth paste and stir into the sauce. Bring to the boil, stirring continuously. Pour some of the sauce into each dish of prunes, leaving about ½ in./1 cm. headspace.

Slice the bananas and toss them gently in the lemon juice. Arrange the banana slices on top of the prunes, dot them with butter and brown under a hot grill. Serve immediately.

COOKING TIME

High/15-lb. pressure 10 minutes
Reduce pressure slowly
Fixed 7½-lb. pressure 20 minutes

Lemon Apricots

 Serves 6

INGREDIENTS	Imperial	Metric	American
Dried apricots	*12 oz.*	*350 g.*	*¾ lb.*
Soft brown sugar	*2 oz.*	*50 g.*	*¼ cup*
Rind and juice 1 lemon			
Sherry (optional)	*2 tbsp.*	*2 tbsp.*	*2 tbsp.*
Flaked almonds	*1 oz.*	*25 g.*	*3 tbsp.*

Place the apricots in a bowl and cover them with boiling water. Cover with a plate and leave for 1 hour. Drain the apricots, reserving the liquid, then arrange them in the pressure cooker (without the trivet). Sprinkle the sugar, lemon rind, lemon juice and sherry over them. Make up the soaking liquid from the apricots to ¾ pt/400 ml./2 cups with water and pour it over the apricots. Bring to pressure and cook for given time. Reduce pressure. Serve hot or cold, scattered with flaked almonds.

COOKING TIME
High/15-lb. pressure 3 minutes
Reduce pressure slowly
Fixed 7½-lb. pressure 5 minutes

Apple and Date Dessert

 Serves 4

INGREDIENTS

	Imperial	Metric	American
Cooking apples, peeled, cored and sliced	1 lb.	450 g.	1 lb.
Demerara or brown sugar	2 oz.	50 g.	$\frac{1}{4}$ cup
Dates, chopped	2 oz.	50 g.	$\frac{1}{4}$ cup
Water	2 tbsp.	2 tbsp.	2 tbsp.
Double or thick cream	$\frac{1}{4}$ pt	150 ml.	$\frac{2}{3}$ cup
Chopped walnuts			

Arrange the apple slices in an ovenproof dish and sprinkle them with the sugar, chopped dates and water. Cover securely with foil. Pour $\frac{1}{2}$ pt/300 ml./$1\frac{1}{4}$ cups water into the pressure cooker. Position the trivet and stand the dish on top. Bring to pressure and cook for given time. Reduce pressure.

Mash the apple mixture with a fork and stir in the cream. Serve hot or cold in individual dishes and decorate with chopped walnuts.

COOKING TIME
Medium/10-lb. pressure 1 minute
Reduce pressure slowly
Fixed 7$\frac{1}{2}$-lb. pressure 2 minutes

Fruit Hat

Serves 4

COOKING TIME
Pre-steaming 15 minutes
Low/5-lb. pressure 40 minutes
Reduce pressure slowly
Fixed 7½-lb. pressure 30 minutes

INGREDIENTS

	Imperial	Metric	American
Self-raising flour	4 oz.	100 g.	1 cup
or flour sifted with 1 tsp. baking powder			
Pinch salt			
Butter, melted	6 oz.	150 g.	¾ cup
White breadcrumbs	4 oz.	100 g.	2 cups
Large egg, beaten	1	1	1
Milk to mix			
Stewed or canned fruit such as blackcurrants, plums, cherries	1 lb.	450 g.	1 lb.
Sugar			

Butter a 1½-pt/1-l./4-cup pudding basin.

Sieve together the flour and salt and mix in the melted butter. Stir in the breadcrumbs and mix to a stiff dough with the beaten egg and a little milk. Roll two-thirds of the dough into a circle and use it to line the prepared basin. Put the strained fruit (sweetened to taste) into the pudding and dampen the edges of the dough. Roll the remaining dough into a circle and place it on top of the pudding, sealing the edges before trimming. Cover securely with foil or a double layer of buttered greaseproof paper.

Pour 1½ pt/1 l./4 cups water into the pressure cooker and position the trivet. Stand the pudding on top. Pre-steam the pudding (see page 83) then bring to pressure and cook for given time. Reduce pressure.

Turn out the pudding. The juice from the strained fruit may be thickened with a little cornflour to make an accompanying sauce.

Fruity Pudding

 Serves 4

INGREDIENTS

	Imperial	Metric	American
Apricot jam	2 tbsp.	2 tbsp.	2 tbsp.
Margarine	3 oz.	75 g	$\frac{1}{3}$ cup
Caster or Superfine sugar	3 oz.	75 g	$\frac{1}{3}$ cup
Grated rind 1 lemon			
Large egg, beaten	1	1	1
Self-raising flour or flour sifted with $1\frac{1}{2}$ tsp. baking powder	6 oz.	150 g.	$1\frac{1}{2}$ cups
Milk to mix			

Butter a 1-pt/600-ml./$2\frac{1}{2}$-cup pudding basin and put the jam in the base. Cream together the margarine, sugar and lemon rind till light and fluffy. Gradually beat in the egg, then fold in the sieved flour. Add a little milk if necessary to make a smooth dropping consistency. Put the mixture into the prepared basin and cover it securely with foil or a double layer of buttered greaseproof paper.

Pour $1\frac{1}{2}$ pt/1 l./4 cups water into the pressure cooker, position the trivet and stand the basin on top. Pre-steam the pudding (see page 83) then bring to pressure and cook for given time. Reduce pressure. Serve with custard.

COOKING TIME
Pre-steaming 15 minutes
Low/5-lb. pressure 25 minutes
Reduce pressure slowly
Fixed $7\frac{1}{2}$-lb. pressure 20 minutes

Chocolate Pudding

 Serves 4

INGREDIENTS

	Imperial	Metric	American
Margarine	2 oz.	50 g.	$\frac{1}{4}$ cup
Caster or Superfine sugar	2 oz.	50 g.	$\frac{1}{4}$ cup
Large egg, beaten	1	1	1
Self-raising flour or flour sifted with $\frac{3}{4}$ tsp. baking powder	3 oz.	75 g.	$\frac{3}{4}$ cup
Cocoa powder	1 tsp.	1 tsp.	1 tsp.
Chopped plain chocolate	2 oz.	50 g.	$\frac{1}{4}$ cup
Milk to mix			

Butter a 1-pt./600-ml./$2\frac{1}{2}$-cup pudding basin. Cream the margarine and sugar till light and fluffy, and gradually beat in the egg. Sieve together the flour and cocoa powder and fold them gently into the mixture along with the chopped chocolate. Add a little milk if necessary to make a smooth dropping consistency. Put the mixture into the prepared basin and cover it securely with foil or a double layer of buttered greaseproof paper.

Pour $1\frac{1}{2}$ pt/1 l./4 cups water into the pressure cooker. Position the trivet and stand the pudding on top. Pre-steam the pudding (see page 83) then bring to pressure and cook for given time. Reduce pressure. Serve with custard or a sweet white sauce.

COOKING TIME
Pre-steaming 25 minutes
Low/5-lb. pressure 25 minutes
Reduce pressure slowly
Fixed $7\frac{1}{2}$-lb. pressure 20 minutes

Raspberry Cream

Serves 4–6

INGREDIENTS

	Imperial	Metric	American
Quantity Egg Custard recipe	See page 86		
Raspberries	1 can	1 can	1 can
Cornflour/cornstarch	1 tbsp.	1 tbsp.	1 tbsp.
Double/thick cream	¼ pt	150 ml.	⅔ cup
Chopped nuts			

Prepare the egg custard, omitting the nutmeg, then cool it slightly. Drain the raspberries and arrange them in a serving bowl. Mix the cornflour with the raspberry juice and bring to the boil, stirring well. Pour this juice over the raspberries and allow it to cool. Stir the cream into the egg custard and pour it over the raspberry mixture. Chill before serving and decorate with chopped nuts.

Christmas Pudding

Makes 2 × 1-lb./450 g. puddings

INGREDIENTS	Imperial	Metric	American
Self-raising flour or flour sifted with $\frac{1}{2}$ tsp. baking powder)	*2 oz.*	*50 g.*	*$\frac{1}{2}$ cup*
Pinch salt			
Each of, grated nutmeg, mixed spice, cinnamon	*$\frac{1}{2}$ tsp.*	*$\frac{1}{2}$ tsp.*	*$\frac{1}{2}$ tsp.*
Fresh white breadcrumbs	*3 oz.*	*75 g.*	*$1\frac{1}{2}$ cups*
Beef suet, shredded or finely chopped	*3 oz.*	*75 g.*	*$\frac{2}{3}$ cup*
Demerara or brown sugar	*2 oz.*	*50 g.*	*$\frac{1}{4}$ cup*
Each, currants, raisins, sultanas, mixed peel	*4 oz.*	*100 g.*	*$\frac{2}{3}$ cup*
Chopped almonds	*1 oz.*	*25 g.*	*$\frac{1}{4}$ cup*
Eggs, beaten	*2*	*2*	*2*
Rind and juice 1 Orange			
Brandy	*2 tbsp.*	*2 tbsp.*	*2 tbsp.*
Milk, ale or stout to mix			

Butter two 1-pt/600-ml./$2\frac{1}{2}$-cup pudding basins. Sieve the flour with the salt and spices. Add all dry ingredients and mix well. Mix together the beaten eggs, orange rind and juice and a little milk. Add these to the fruit mixture and stir well. Turn into the prepared basins and cover securely with foil or a double layer of buttered greaseproof paper. Pour $2\frac{1}{2}$ pt/$1\frac{1}{2}$ l./$6\frac{1}{2}$ cups water into the pressure cooker and position the trivet. Stand the puddings on the trivet. Pre-steam the puddings for the time shown then bring to pressure and cook for given time. Reduce pressure. Serve with brandy sauce.

COOKING TIME
Pre-steaming 20 minutes
High/15-lb. pressure $1\frac{3}{4}$ hours
Reduce pressure slowly
Fixed $7\frac{1}{2}$-lb. pressure $2\frac{1}{2}$ hours

REHEATING TIME
High/15-lb. pressure 20 minutes
Reduce pressure slowly
Fixed $7\frac{1}{2}$-lb. pressure 40 minutes

CHECKPOINT

The puddings should be prepared in October so that they have time to mature before Christmas. If your pressure cooker is large enough, cook the puddings side by side on the trivet, or one on top of the other with the trivet between. The basins must not touch the sides or the lid.

Spiced Fruit Pudding

 Serves 4

INGREDIENTS

	Imperial	Metric	American
Self-raising flour	4 oz.	100 g.	1 cup
or flour sifted with			
1 tsp. baking powder			
Pinch salt			
Cinnamon	2 tsp.	2 tsp.	2 tsp.
Grated nutmeg	1 tsp.	1 tsp.	1 tsp.
Butter	3 oz.	75 g.	⅓ cup
Caster or Superfine sugar	3 oz.	75 g.	⅓ cup
Brown breadcrumbs	4 oz.	100 g.	2 cups
Mixed dried fruit	4 oz.	100 g.	⅔ cup
Grated nutmeg	1 tsp.	1 tsp.	1 tsp.
Egg, beaten	1	1	1
Milk to mix			

Butter a 1½-pt./1-l./4-cup pudding basin.

Sieve together the flour, salt, cinnamon and nutmeg, then rub in the butter till the mixture resembles fine breadcrumbs. Stir in the sugar, breadcrumbs and fruit. Mix in the beaten egg, adding a little milk if necessary to make a smooth dropping consistency. Put the mixture into the prepared basin and cover securely with foil or a double layer of buttered greaseproof paper. Pour 1½ pt/1 l./4 cups water into the pressure cooker (2½ pt/1½ l./6½ cups if fixed 7½-lb pressure), position the trivet and stand the basin on top. Pre-steam the pudding (see page 83), then bring to pressure and cook for given time. Reduce pressure. Serve with cream or custard.

COOKING TIMES

Pre-steaming 25 minutes
High/15-lb. pressure 45 minutes
Reduce pressure slowly
Fixed 7½-lb. pressure 1 hour 20 minutes

Quick-Baked Apples

 Serves 4

INGREDIENTS

	Imperial	Metric	American
Soft brown sugar	2 oz.	50 g.	¼ cup
Cinnamon	½ tsp.	½ tsp.	½ tsp.
Pinch ground cloves			
Sultanas	4 oz.	100 g.	⅔ cup
Juice ½ lemon			
Medium cooking apples,	4	4	4
cored			

Mix together the sugar, cinnamon, cloves, sultanas and lemon juice. Pack the core hollows of the apples tightly with the mixture. Pour ½ pt/300 ml./1¼ cups water into the pressure cooker and position the trivet. Stand the apples on top, bring to pressure and cook for given time. Reduce pressure.

Arrange the apples on a serving dish and serve with cream or custard.

COOKING TIME

High/15-lb. pressure 4 minutes
Reduce pressure slowly
Fixed 7½-lb. pressure 10 minutes

Bread and Butter Pudding

 Serves 4

INGREDIENTS

	Imperial	Metric	American
Sliced buttered bread, cut into triangles	*4–6*	*4–6*	*4–6*
Sultanas	*2 oz.*	*50 g.*	*$\frac{1}{3}$ cup*
Currants	*2 oz.*	*50 g.*	*$\frac{1}{3}$ cup*
Caster or Superfine sugar	*1 oz.*	*25 g.*	*2 tbsp.*
Milk	*$\frac{3}{4}$ pt*	*400 ml.*	*2 cups*
Large eggs, beaten	*2*	*2*	*2*
Grated nutmeg			

Butter a suitable ovenproof dish and layer the bread triangles in the dish with the sultanas, currants and sugar. Warm the milk and pour on to the beaten eggs, stirring well. Pour this mixture over the bread and sprinkle it with grated nutmeg. Cover the basin securely with foil or a double layer of buttered greaseproof paper. Pour 1 pt/600 ml./$2\frac{1}{2}$ cups water into the pressure cooker. Position the trivet and stand the basin on top. Bring to pressure and cook for given time. Reduce pressure. Brown under a hot grill to serve.

COOKING TIME

High/15-lb. pressure 6 minutes
Reduce pressure slowly
Fixed $7\frac{1}{2}$-lb. pressure 15 minutes

Somerset Pears

 Serves 4

INGREDIENTS

	Imperial	Metric	American
Medium pears, peeled, halved	*4*	*4*	*4*
Caster or Superfine sugar	*2 tbsp.*	*2 tbsp.*	*2 tbsp.*
Cider	*$\frac{1}{4}$ pt*	*150 ml*	*$\frac{2}{3}$ cup*
Water	*$\frac{1}{4}$ pt*	*150 ml.*	*$\frac{2}{3}$ cup*
Juice 1 orange			
Apple jelly	*2 tbsp.*	*2 tbsp.*	*2 tbsp.*
Cloves	*2*	*2*	*2*

Place the pear halves in the pressure cooker (without the trivet) and sprinkle the sugar over the pears. Add remaining ingredients, bring to pressure and cook for given time. Reduce pressure. Arrange the pears and liquor in a serving dish and chill them. Serve with ice cream.

COOKING TIME

High/15-lb. pressure 4–8 minutes
Reduce pressure with cold water
Fixed $7\frac{1}{2}$-lb. pressure 8–12 minutes

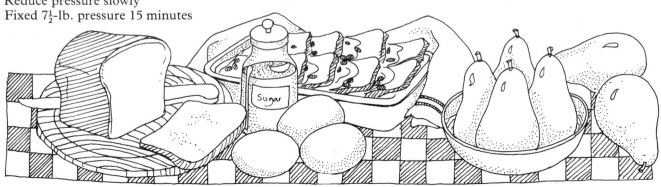

ALL-IN-ONE-MEALS

All-in-one meals are simple to prepare in the pressure cooker. There are of course recipes in this book which can be prepared as meals in themselves. The majority of the meat, poultry and game recipes need only vegetables cooked along with the main ingredients to make a complete meal.

In this section I have made particular use of rice. It may be cooked in the pressure cooker with other ingredients or separately, as you will see.

All-in-one meals are particularly suitable when a quick meal is required and/or when only one cooking ring is available.

Boiled Beef and Dumplings

Serves 4–6

INGREDIENTS

	Imperial	Metric	American
Cooking oil	2 tbsp.	2 tbsp.	2 tbsp.
Brisket, rolled	2½ lb.	1.1 kg.	2½ lb.
Carrots	4	4	4
Small onions	4	4	4
Beef stock	1 pt	500 ml.	2½ cups
Bay leaves	2	2	2
Good pinch mace			
Salt and pepper			
Dumplings:			
Self-raising flour or flour sifted with ½ tsp. baking powder	4 oz.	100 g.	1 cup
Shredded or finely chopped suet	2 oz.	50 g.	½ cup
Small onion, finely chopped	1	1	1
Salt and pepper			
Chopped parsley	1 tbsp.	1 tbsp.	1 tbsp.
Cold water	4 tbsp.	4 tbsp.	4 tbsp.

Heat the cooking oil in the open pressure cooker and brown the beef well on all sides. Arrange the whole carrots and onions around the meat and pour in the beef stock. Add the bay leaves, mace and seasoning. Bring to pressure and cook for given time. Reduce pressure.

Mix together the ingredients for the dumplings, forming the soft dough into eight balls. Return the open pan to the heat and place the dumplings around the meat. Place the lid on the pressure cooker *without the weight or valve* and simmer the dumplings for 10–15 minutes.

Place the meat on a serving dish with the vegetables and the dumplings. Thicken the stock if liked with a little cornflour mixed with cold water and serve it separately.

COOKING TIME
High/15-lb. pressure 30 minutes
Reduce pressure slowly
Fixed 7½-lb. pressure 60 minutes

TO FREEZE
Leftover slices of beef may be put in a foil tray with gravy poured over them, then frozen.

Beef Curry

 ❊ Serves 4

INGREDIENTS

	Imperial	Metric	American
Butter	*3 oz.*	*75 g.*	*⅓ cup*
Each, ground coriander, cumin, chillies, cardamon, turmeric	*1½ tsp.*	*1½ tsp.*	*1½ tsp.*
Each, ground ginger, fenugreek, pepper, mixed spice	*½ tsp.*	*½ tsp.*	*½ tsp.*
Clove garlic, crushed	*1*	*1*	*1*
Cinnamon stick	*1*	*1*	*1*
Bay leaf	*1*	*1*	*1*
Large onion, chopped	*1*	*1*	*1*
Stewing steak, cut into cubes	*1½ lb.*	*700 g.*	*1½ lb.*
Beef stock	*½ pt*	*300 ml.*	*1¼ cups*
or for 7½-lb. pressure	*¾ pt*	*400 ml.*	*2 cups*
Juice ½ lemon			
Caster/Superfine sugar	*1 tbsp.*	*1 tbsp.*	*1 tbsp.*
Long-grain rice	*8 oz.*	*225 g.*	*1–1¼ cups*
Slightly salted boiling water	*¾ pt*	*400 ml.*	*2 cups*

Heat the butter in the open pressure cooker and in it fry the dry spices gently with the garlic for 2–3 minutes. Add the onion and sauté it until soft. Add the cubes of meat and stir till they are covered with spices and beginning to brown.

Stir in the remaining ingredients, except the rice and water, bring to pressure and cook for given time. Reduce pressure.

Put the rice into an ovenproof basin, pour the boiling water over it and cover securely with foil. Place the trivet on the meat and stand the basin on the trivet. Bring to pressure again and cook for given time. Reduce pressure.

Fluff up the rice with a fork to separate the grains and arrange it on a serving dish.

Remove the bay leaf and cinnamon stick from the curry. If liked, the curry may be thickened with a little cornflour mixed with cold water. Spoon the curry into the centre of the rice. Serve with some of the following: thinly-sliced tomato and onion; sliced bananas, sprinkled with lemon juice; cucumber cubes dressed with natural yoghurt; chutney.

COOKING TIME

High/15-lb. pressure curry 15 minutes
Reduce pressure with cold water
    rice added 5 minutes
Reduce pressure slowly
Fixed 7½-lb. pressure curry 30 minutes
    rice added 10 minutes

TO FREEZE

Pack the curry in a rigid polythene container, cover and freeze. Cook rice just before serving.

Note: This is one of my favourite curry recipes. If preferred, the dry spices may be replaced with 2–3 tbsp. curry powder.

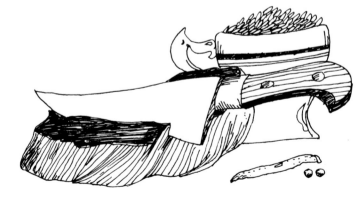

Bacon Pilaff

 Serves 4

INGREDIENTS	Imperial	Metric	American
Butter	*2 oz.*	*50 g.*	*¼ cup*
Onions, chopped	*2*	*2*	*2*
Lean, thick-cut bacon, chopped	*8 oz.*	*225 g.*	*½ lb.*
Shelled peanuts	*1 oz.*	*25 g.*	*¼ cup*
Long-grain rice	*8 oz.*	*225 g.*	*1–1¼ cup*
Currants	*2 oz.*	*50 g.*	*⅓ cup*
Tomatoes, skinned and chopped	*2*	*2*	*2*
Onion stock	*1 pt*	*550 ml.*	*2½ cups*
(If 7½-lb. pressure)	*1¼ pt*	*700 ml.*	*3 cups*
Mixed spice	*½ tsp.*	*½ tsp.*	*½ tsp.*
Salt and pepper			
Chopped parsley	*1 tbsp.*	*1 tbsp.*	*1 tbsp.*

Heat the butter in the open pressure cooker and in it sauté the onions and bacon gently for 2–3 minutes. Stir in the remaining ingredients, except the parsley, bring to pressure and cook for given time. Reduce pressure.

Fluff up the rice with a fork to separate the grains, stir in the chopped parsley and serve.

COOKING TIME
High/15-lb. pressure 5 minutes
Reduce pressure slowly
Fixed 7½-lb. pressure 8–10 minutes
Allow pressure cooker to stand for a minute before opening, place under cold water.

Chicken Risotto

 Serves 4

INGREDIENTS	Imperial	Metric	American
Butter	*3 oz.*	*75 g.*	*⅓ cup*
Onions, chopped	*2*	*2*	*2*
Clove garlic, crushed (optional)	*1*	*1*	*1*
Green pepper, de-seeded and chopped	*1*	*1*	*1*
Mushrooms, sliced	*4 oz.*	*100 g.*	*¼ lb.*
Cooked chicken, chopped	*8 oz.*	*225 g.*	*½ lb.*
Long-grain rice	*8 oz.*	*225 g.*	*1–1¼ cup*
White wine	*¼ pt*	*150 ml.*	*⅔ cup*
Chicken stock	*¾ pt*	*400 ml.*	*2 cups*
(If 7½-lb. pressure)	*1 pt*	*550 ml.*	*2½ cups*
Salt and pepper			
Grated Parmesan cheese			

Heat the butter in the open pressure cooker and sauté the onions, garlic, pepper and mushrooms for a few minutes. Stir in the cooked chicken, rice, wine and chicken stock. Season to taste. Bring to pressure and cook for given time. Reduce pressure.

Place the open pressure cooker on a gentle heat and fluff up the rice with a fork to separate the grains. Sprinkle with Parmesan cheese and serve.

COOKING TIME
High/15-lb. pressure 5 minutes
Reduce pressure slowly
Fixed 7½-lb. pressure 8–10 minutes
Allow to stand for a minute before opening, place under cold water.

Note: Risotto may be made using any cooked meat or fish.

Vegetable Hotpot

 Serves 4

INGREDIENTS

	Imperial	Metric	American
Dried butter beans	4 oz.	100 g.	$\frac{1}{4}$ lb.
Butter	1 oz.	25 g.	2 tbsp.
Large onion, sliced	1	1	1
Carrots, sliced	8 oz.	225 g.	$\frac{1}{2}$ lb.
Dried mixed herbs	$\frac{1}{2}$ tsp.	$\frac{1}{2}$ tsp.	$\frac{1}{2}$ tsp.
Stock			
Salt and pepper			
Short macaroni	4 oz.	100 g.	$\frac{1}{4}$ lb.
Frozen peas	4 oz.	100 g.	$\frac{1}{4}$ lb.
Croûtes:			
Butter	1 oz.	25 g.	2 tbsp.
Cheddar cheese, grated	2 oz.	50 g.	$\frac{1}{2}$ cup
Made mustard	1 tsp.	1 tsp.	1 tsp.
Thick slices French bread	4	4	4

Place the butter beans in a large dish and cover with plenty of boiling water. Cover with a plate and leave for 1 hour. Heat the butter in the open pressure cooker and in it sauté the onion, carrots and herbs gently for 3–4 minutes. Drain the butter beans and add these to the pressure cooker. Make up the soaking liquid from the beans to 1 pt/550 ml./2$\frac{1}{2}$ cups with stock. Add this to the bean mixture and season with salt and pepper. Bring to pressure and cook for given time. Reduce pressure.

Add the macaroni and frozen peas to the vegetables, bring to pressure again and cook for given time. Reduce pressure. Pour the vegetables into a casserole dish.

Beat together the softened butter, cheese and mustard and spread on to one side of the bread slices. Place the bread, butter side up, on top of the casserole. Place under a hot grill until the cheese melts. Serve more cheese separately.

COOKING TIME
High/15-lb. pressure 15 minutes
Reduce pressure slowly
  macaroni added 5 minutes
Reduce pressure slowly
Fixed 7$\frac{1}{2}$-lb. pressure 30 minutes
  macaroni added 10 minutes

TO FREEZE
Pack in rigid polythene container, cover and freeze. Thaw completely before reheating. Add croûtes on reheating.

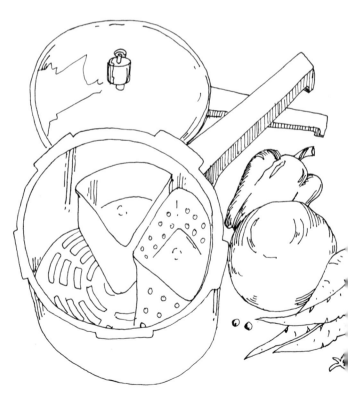

Old Fashioned Beef Casserole

 Serves 4–6

INGREDIENTS	Imperial	Metric	American
Lard or dripping	1 oz.	25 g.	2 tbsp.
Stewing steak, cut into cubes	1½ lb.	700 g.	1½ lb.
Onions, sliced	2	2	2
Carrots, sliced	2	2	2
Leeks, sliced	2	2	2
Celery, sliced	2 sticks	2 sticks	2 stalks
Small swede, sliced	½	½	½
Large potatoes, quatered	2	2	2
Beef stock	1 pt	600 ml.	2½ cups
Salt and pepper			
Bouquet garni			

Heat the lard or dripping in the open pressure cooker and in it brown the meat for 4–5 minutes. Lift out with a draining spoon. In the same fat sauté the vegetables gently for 3–4 minutes, then stir in the browned meat, beef stock, seasoning and bouquet garni. Bring to pressure and cook for given time. Reduce pressure. Remove bouquet garni.

COOKING TIME

High/15-lb. pressure 15 minutes
Reduce pressure slowly
Fixed 7½-lb. pressure 35 minutes

Kedgeree

 Serves 4

INGREDIENTS	Imperial	Metric	American
Long-grain rice	8 oz.	225 g.	1–1¼ cup
Boiling water, slightly salted	¾ pt	400 ml.	2 cups
Smoked haddock fillets	1¼ lb.	600 g.	1¼ lb.
Salt and pepper			
Butter	2 oz.	50 g.	¼ cup
Hard-boiled eggs, chopped	2	2	2
Single or thin cream	¼ pt	150 ml.	⅔ cup
Chopped parsley			

Place the rice in an ovenproof basin and pour on the boiling water. Cover securely with foil. Pour ½ pt/300 ml./1¼ cups of water into the pressure cooker and position the trivet. Stand the bowl of rice on the trivet and arrange the seasoned haddock fillets around. Bring to pressure and cook for given time. Reduce pressure.

Remove the bowl of rice, haddock, trivet and water, and wipe the inside of the pressure cooker with kitchen paper. Fluff up the rice with a fork to separate the grains and flake the haddock.

Heat the butter in the open pressure cooker and stir in the rice, fish, chopped hard-boiled eggs and cream. Heat through gently and adjust seasoning if necessary. Serve garnished with chopped parsley.

COOKING TIME

High/15-lb. pressure 5 minutes
Reduce pressure with cold water
Fixed 7½-lb. pressure 10 minutes

ENTERTAINING

The pressure cooker is superb for entertaining, taking much of the time and effort out of preparing delicious food for your guests – quite an advantage when life is so busy. Entertaining can be an expensive pastime, but it is satisfying to know that you are saving a considerable amount of fuel.

Dishes can be pre-cooked in advance of the meal (then frozen?) and served cold or reheated just before serving. Perhaps the starter and the dessert could be prepared in advance, leaving only the main course to be cooked on the day.

Many recipes in this book are suitable for entertaining and I hope you will have pleasure in menu planning. The menus and recipes in this section are intended to serve simply as guide-lines to efficient entertaining.

Make full use of your pressure cooker over the Christmas holidays, and you will find that you have more time to relax and enjoy yourself with family and friends. This is an ideal time to cook nourishing soups to warm up winter evenings.

For Christmas lunch try serving a fruit soup or cold vegetable soup, prepared in the pressure cooker, of course. Save yourself some washing up by cooking all the vegetables together (or in two batches if you have a large number of guests) in the pressure cooker. While you sit down to enjoy the main course the Christmas pud' can be reheating in the pressure cooker.

Use up leftover turkey, game etc. in pressure-cooked soups, pilaf, risotto and so on.

Dinner for 4

Pork & Bacon Pâté

Beef Bourguignon, with green salad

Crème Brûlée

Pork and Bacon Paté

Serves 8–10

INGREDIENTS

	Imperial	Metric	American
Streaky bacon	8 oz.	225 g.	½ lb.
Pork, minced	1 lb.	450 g.	1 lb.
Small onion, minced	1	1	1
White breadcrumbs	6 oz.	175 g.	3 cups
Mushrooms, finely chopped	2 oz.	50 g.	½ cup
Salt	2 tsp.	2 tsp.	2 tsp.
Black pepper	1 tsp.	1 tsp.	1 tsp.
Ground mace	2 tsp.	2 tsp.	2 tsp.
Eggs, beaten	2	2	2

Remove the rind from the bacon and stretch the bacon with the blade of a knife. Use it to line a suitable ovenproof container (about 6 in./15 cm. diameter). Mix together the remaining ingredients and press them firmly into the prepared container, folding the ends of the bacon on to the pâté. Cover securely with foil. Pour 1 pt/600 ml./2½ cups water into the pressure cooker (1½ pt/1 l./3¾ cups if fixed 7½-lb. pressure) and position the trivet. Stand the pâté on top. Bring to pressure and cook for given time. Reduce pressure.

Put a plate on top of the pâté and weight it down. Allow it to cool like this before turning it out. Serve in slices with crisp fingers of toast.

COOKING TIME

High/15-lb. pressure 25 minutes
Reduce pressure slowly
Fixed 7½-lb. pressure 50 minutes

TO FREEZE

The pâté is best frozen in slices, interleaved with polythene and wrapped in foil.

Beef Bourguignon

Serves 4

INGREDIENTS

	Imperial	Metric	American
Butter	2 oz.	50 g.	¼ cup
Chuck steak, cut into cubes	1¾ lb.	800 g.	1¾ lb.
Onions, chopped	2	2	2
Clove garlic, crushed	1	1	1
Streaky bacon, chopped	4 oz.	100 g.	¼ lb.
Red wine	1 pt	550 ml.	2½ cups
Bouquet garni			
Salt and pepper			
Button mushrooms	8 oz.	225 g.	½ lb.
Flour	2–3 tbsp.	2–3 tbsp.	2–3 tbsp.
Chopped parsley			

Heat the butter in the open pressure cooker and in it brown the meat for 3–4 minutes. Lift it out with a draining spoon. In the same butter sauté the onions, garlic and bacon gently till transparent. Return the meat to the pressure cooker and add the red wine, bouquet garni, seasoning and mushrooms. Bring to pressure and cook for given time. Reduce pressure. Remove bouquet garni.

Mix the flour with a little cold water to form a smooth paste and add to the beef. Bring to the boil, stirring well. Garnish with chopped parsley and serve with plenty of green salad.

COOKING TIME

High/15-lb. pressure 20 minutes
Reduce pressure slowly
Fixed 7½-lb. pressure 45 minutes

TO FREEZE

Omit garlic, pack into rigid polythene container, cover and freeze. Add garlic at reheating stage. Alternatively season well with garlic salt.

Crème Brûlée

Serves 4

INGREDIENTS

	Imperial	Metric	American
Single or thin cream	$\frac{1}{2}$ pt	300 ml.	1$\frac{1}{4}$ cups
Double or thick cream	$\frac{1}{2}$ pt	300 ml.	1$\frac{1}{4}$ cups
Egg yolks	4	4	4
Vanilla essence	1 tsp.	1 tsp.	1 tsp.
Caster or Superfine sugar	4–5 tbsp.	4–5 tbsp.	4–5 tbsp.

Butter an ovenproof serving dish. Heat the single and double creams together in a saucepan (but do not allow to boil). Mix together the egg yolks, vanilla essence and 1 tbsp. of the sugar, and pour the warmed cream over the eggs. Pour the mixture into the prepared dish and cover it securely with foil.

Pour $\frac{1}{2}$ pt/300 ml./1$\frac{1}{4}$ cups water into the pressure cooker with the trivet. Stand the dish on the trivet. Bring to pressure and cook for given time. Reduce pressure.

Chill the cream for several hours or preferably overnight. Pre-heat the grill. Dust the top of the cream evenly with the remaining sugar and place it under the grill (at least 4 in./10 cm. away) so the sugar melts and begins to brown. Chill for 2–3 hours before serving.

This rich dessert is delicious served with sugared fresh fruit.

COOKING TIME
High/15-lb. pressure 5 minutes
Reduce pressure slowly
Fixed 7$\frac{1}{2}$-lb. pressure 10 minutes

Lunch or Dinner for 6

Vichyssoise

Duck with Almonds, with new potatoes and green beans

Pears in Red Wine

Vichyssoise

 Serves 6

INGREDIENTS	Imperial	Metric	American
Butter	3 oz.	75 g.	⅓ cup
Leeks, sliced	6	6	6
Onions, sliced	2	2	2
Potatoes, thinly sliced	2	2	2
Salt and pepper			
Chicken stock	1¾ pt	1 l.	4½ cups
Sprigs parsley	2–3	2–3	2–3
Single or thin cream	½ pt	300 ml.	1¼ cups
Chopped chives to garnish			

Heat the butter in the open pressure cooker and in it sauté the vegetables for 2–3 minutes without browning them. Season and add the chicken stock and parsley sprigs. Bring to pressure and cook for given time. Reduce pressure.

Remove parsley sprigs. Liquidize or sieve the soup and cool it. Stir the cream into the chilled soup just before serving it garnished with chopped chives.

COOKING TIME
High/15-lb. pressure 6 minutes
Reduce pressure slowly
Fixed 7½-lb. pressure 15 minutes

TO FREEZE
Pack in rigid polythene container, cover and freeze. Add cream and chives just before serving.

Note: This soup may also be served hot with the cream stirred in just before serving.

Duck with Almonds

 Serves 6

INGREDIENTS	Imperial	Metric	American
Duck portions	6	6	6
Seasoned flour			
Butter	1 oz.	25 g.	2 tbsp.
Cooking oil	1 tbsp.	1 tbsp.	1 tbsp.
Spring onions, sliced	4 oz.	100 g.	¼ lb.
Split toasted almonds	4 oz.	225 g.	1 cup
Dry white wine	1 pt	600 ml.	2½ cups
(If 7½ lb. pressure)	1¼ pt	700 ml.	3 cups
Chopped parsley			

Coat the duck portions with seasoned flour. Heat the butter and oil in the open pressure cooker and in it sauté the duck all over till golden brown. Sprinkle the onions and almonds over the duck, then pour on the wine. Bring to pressure and cook for given time. Reduce pressure.

Remove surface fat with kitchen paper if necessary. Arrange the duck and sauce in a serving dish and garnish with chopped parsley. Serve with tiny new potatoes and green beans, pressure-cooked just before serving.

COOKING TIME
High/15-lb. 12 minutes
Reduce pressure slowly
Fixed 7½-lb. pressure 25 minutes

Pears in Red Wine

 Serves 6

INGREDIENTS

	Imperial	Metric	American
Medium pears, peeled, halved and cored	6	6	6
Caster or Superfine sugar	3 oz.	75 g.	6 tbsp.
Juice ½ lemon			
Red-currant jelly	4 tbsp.	4 tbsp.	4 tbsp.
Red wine	¾ pt	400 ml.	2 cups
Whipped cream			

Arrange the pear halves in the pressure cooker (without the trivet) and sprinkle with the sugar and lemon juice. Add the red-currant jelly and the red wine, bring to pressure and cook for given time. Reduce pressure.

Arrange the pears in a serving dish and pour the juice over and around them. Chill, decorate with whipped cream and serve.

COOKING TIME
High/15-lb. pressure 4–8 minutes
Reduce pressure with cold water
Fixed 7½-lb. pressure 8–12 minutes

Supper for 8

Chilli Beans, with crusty French bread and salad

Baked potatoes

Peach Compote, with macaroons

Chilli Beans

 Serves 8

INGREDIENTS

	Imperial	Metric	American
Dried red kidney beans	1 lb.	450 g.	1 lb.
Cooking oil	2 tbsp.	2 tbsp.	2 tbsp.
Butter	1 oz.	25 g.	2 tbsp.
Minced beef hamburgers	2 lb.	1 kg.	2 lb.
Large onions, chopped	2	2	2
Canned tomatoes	14-oz.	397-g.	1 lb.
Salt and pepper			
Vinegar	2 tbsp.	2 tbsp.	2 tbsp.
Sugar	2 tbsp.	2 tbsp.	2 tbsp.
Chilli powder	1–1½ tbsp.	1–1½ tbsp.	1–1½ tbsp.
Beef stock			

Place the beans in a large bowl and cover them with boiling water. Cover with a plate and leave for 1 hour.

Heat the oil and butter in the open pressure cooker and in it lightly brown the minced beef. Add the onions, strained beans and tomatoes, including the juice. Make up the soaking liquid from the beans to 1 pt /550 ml./2½ cups with beef stock (1¼ pt/700 ml./3 cups if fixed 7½-lb. pressure) and add it to the mince. Make sure the pressure cooker is not more than half full. Bring to pressure and cook for given time. Reduce pressure.

If necessary, boil the mixture for a few minutes in the open pressure cooker to reduce and thicken the liquid.

Serve with crusty French bread and baked potatoes. The potatoes' cooking time may be shortened by partially cooking them in the pressure cooker. Scrub the potatoes and prick the skins with a fork. Pour ½ pt/300 ml./1¼ cups of water into the pressure cooker with the trivet (1 pt/500 ml./2½ cups if fixed 7½-lb. pressure) and stand the potatoes on top. Bring to pressure and cook for 10 minutes at High/15-lb. pressure or 20 minutes at 7½-lb. pressure. Reduce pressure. Sprinkle the potatoes with salt and crisp them up for 30–45 minutes in a hot oven.

COOKING TIME

High/15-lb. pressure 15 minutes
Reduce pressure slowly
Fixed 7½-lb. pressure 30 minutes

Peach Compote

Serves 8

INGREDIENTS

	Imperial	Metric	American
Peaches, peeled, halved and stoned	8	8	8
Red wine	¾ pt	400 ml.	2 cups
Oranges, grated rind and juice	2	2	2
Flaked almonds	2 tbsp.	2 tbsp.	2 tbsp.
Sugar			

Arrange the peach halves in the pressure cooker and add the red wine, orange rind and juice, and flaked almonds. If liked, sweeten with a little sugar. Bring to pressure and cook for given time. Reduce pressure.

Serve chilled with macaroons.

COOKING TIME

High/15-lb. pressure 4 minutes
Reduce pressure with cold water
Fixed 7½-lb. pressure 8 minutes

PRESERVES

If you are a lover of home-made preserves, your pressure cooker will be a great time-saver. Marmalades, jams, jellies and chutneys can all be prepared in the pressure cooker.

Fruit for marmalades, jams and jellies is softened under pressure. When the sugar is added, the pressure cooker is used like an ordinary saucepan (without the lid) until the preserve reaches setting point.

Chutney ingredients are cooked under pressure, then reduced and thickened in the open pressure cooker for potting.

MARMALADES, JAMS AND JELLIES

When softening fruit under pressure, fill the pressure cooker no more than half full.

The trivet is not used.

Choose fresh, ripe, firm, unblemished fruit for a good result.

Softening the fruit helps to release the pectin (the setting agent) in fruit. Some fruits contain more than others, and you may need to mix fruits or to add lemon to compensate.

High-pectin fruits: damsons, blackcurrants, redcurrants, gooseberries.

Medium-pectin fruits: apricots, greengages, loganberries, plums, raspberries.

Low-pectin fruits: blackberries, cherries, marrow, pears, rhubarb, strawberries.

Warmed sugar will take less time to dissolve and will produce a preserve of better colour and flavour.

Once the sugar has been added the lid *must not* be replaced on the pressure cooker. Use the pressure cooker base as an ordinary pan.

There are three methods of checking that the jam has reached setting point:
1. The temperature test is the most accurate method. The jam will set when it reaches a temperature of 221°F. (104°C).
2. Place a little of the jam on to a cold plate. When the jam is cool, push your finger across its surface. If it wrinkles, you have a set. During this test remember to move the pressure cooker off the heat to avoid boiling the jam too long.
3. Stir the jam with a wooden spoon and lift it out. The jam will begin to set on the spoon when setting point is reached.

When adapting you own recipes for pressure-cooking, reduce the liquid by about half (but make sure you include the minimum amount recommended in your instruction book). Generally, allow 1 lb./450 g. sugar per 1 lb./450 g. fruit.

Apple Chutney

Makes about 4 lb./1.8 kg.

INGREDIENTS	Imperial	Metric	American
Cooking apples, peeled, cored and diced	2 lb.	1 kg.	2 lb.
Onions, chopped	2 lb.	1 kg.	2 lb.
Sultanas	4 oz.	100 g.	$\frac{1}{4}$ lb.
Malt vinegar	$\frac{1}{2}$ pt	300 ml.	1$\frac{1}{4}$ cups
(If 7$\frac{1}{2}$-lb. pressure)	$\frac{3}{4}$ pt	400 ml.	2 cups
Lemon, grated rind and juice	1	1	1
Ground cloves	1 tsp.	1 tsp.	1 tsp.
Ground cinnamon	1 tsp.	1 tsp.	1 tsp.
Ground ginger	1 tsp.	1 tsp.	1 tsp.
Salt	1 tsp.	1 tsp.	1 tsp.
Demerara/brown sugar	12 oz.	350 g.	$\frac{3}{4}$ lb.

Place the apples, onions and sultanas in the pressure cooker with the vinegar (without the trivet). Bring to pressure and cook for given time. Reduce pressure. Add the remaining ingredients and heat them gently until the sugar dissolves. Bring to the boil and simmer in the open pressure cooker until the chutney thickens. Pour into warm, dry jars, cover and label.

COOKING TIME

High/15-lb. pressure 12 minutes
Reduce pressure slowly
Fixed 7$\frac{1}{2}$-lb. pressure 25 minutes

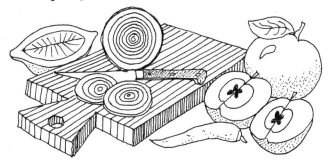

Rhubarb Chutney

Makes 3 lb./1.4 kg.

INGREDIENTS	Imperial	Metric	American
Rhubarb, sliced	3 lb.	1.4 kg.	3 lb.
Onions, chopped	8 oz.	225 g.	$\frac{1}{2}$ lb.
Ground ginger	1 tsp.	1 tsp.	1 tsp.
Mixed spice	2 tsp.	2 tsp.	2 tsp.
Salt	1 tsp.	1 tsp.	1 tsp.
Malt vinegar	$\frac{3}{4}$ pt	400 ml.	2 cups
(If 7$\frac{1}{2}$-lb. pressure)	1 pt	550 ml.	2$\frac{1}{2}$ cups
Sugar	1 lb.	450 g.	1 lb.

Place all the ingredients, except the sugar, in the pressure cooker (without the trivet). Bring to pressure and cook for given time. Reduce pressure.

Add the sugar and heat it gently till it dissolves. Bring to the boil and simmer gently in the open pressure cooker until the chutney thickens. Pour into warm, dry jars, cover and label.

COOKING TIME

High/15-lb. pressure 4 minutes
Reduce pressure slowly
Fixed 7$\frac{1}{2}$-lb. pressure 8 minutes

Green Tomato Chutney

Makes about 3 lb./1.4 kg.

INGREDIENTS

	Imperial	Metric	American
Green tomatoes, thinly sliced	3 lb.	1.4 kg.	3 lb.
Onions, chopped	8 oz.	225 g.	½ lb.
Cooking apples, peeled, cored and chopped	1 lb.	450 g.	1 lb.
Sultanas	8 oz.	225 g.	½ lb.
Salt	2 tbsp.	2 tbsp.	2 tbsp.
Malt vinegar	¾ pt	400 ml.	2 cups
(If 7½-lb. pressure)	1 pt	550 ml.	2½ cups
Dry mustard	1 tsp.	1 tsp.	1 tsp.
Ground ginger	1 tsp.	1 tsp.	1 tsp.
Cayenne pepper	½ tsp.	½ tsp.	½ tsp.
Demerara/brown sugar	8 oz.	225 g.	½ lb.

Place all the ingredients, except the sugar, in the pressure cooker (without the trivet). Bring to pressure and cook for given time. Reduce pressure.

Add the sugar and heat gently till it dissolves. Bring to the boil and simmer gently in the open pressure cooker until the chutney thickens. Pour into warm dry jars, cover and label.

COOKING TIME
High/15-lb. pressure 10 minutes
Reduce pressure slowly
Fixed 7½-lb. pressure 25 minutes

Lemon Curd

Makes about 2 lb./1 kg.

INGREDIENTS

	Imperial	Metric	American
Eggs, beaten	4	4	4
Sugar	1 lb.	450 g.	1 lb.
Lemons, finely-grated rind	4	4	4
Lemons, strained juice	2	2	2
Butter, cut into small pieces	4 oz.	100 g.	¼ lb.

Strain the beaten eggs into an ovenproof basin and stir in the sugar, lemon rind, lemon juice and butter pieces. Securely tie on a double layer of buttered greaseproof paper. Pour ½ pt/300 ml./1¼ cups water into the pressure cooker (1 pt/500 ml./2¼ cups if fixed 7½-lb. pressure) and position the trivet. Stand the basin on the trivet, bring to pressure and cook for given time. Reduce pressure. Stir the lemon curd and pour into warm, dry jars. Cool, cover and label.

COOKING TIME
High/15-lb. pressure 10 minutes
Reduce pressure slowly
Fixed 7½-lb. pressure 25 minutes

Note: Lemon Curd may be stored for up to 2 months only.

Orange Marmalade

Makes 4–5 lb./1.8–2.2 kg.

INGREDIENTS

	Imperial	Metric	American
Seville oranges	1½ lb.	700 g.	1½ lb.
Water	1 pt	550 ml.	2½ cups
(If 7½-lb. pressure)	1¼ pt	700 ml.	3 cups
Juice 1 lemon			
Sugar	3 lb.	1.4 kg.	3 lb.

Remove the peel from the oranges, using a sharp knife or potato peeler and making sure no pith is attached. Cut the peel into pieces. Cut the oranges in half and squeeze out the juice. Tie the pith and pips in a piece of muslin and soak in the water overnight. Place the water, muslin bag, peel and lemon juice in the pressure cooker. Bring to pressure and cook for given time. Reduce pressure.

Cool the liquid sufficiently to squeeze the juice from the muslin bag into the orange liquor. Stir in the sugar. Discard the muslin bag. Heat the marmalade gently until the sugar dissolves, then boil it rapidly in the open pressure cooker until setting point is reached (see page 108). To prevent the peel rising in the jars, cool the marmalade until a skin begins to form (about 15 minutes), then pour it into warm, dry jars and cover with wax discs. When cool, cover and label.

COOKING TIME

High/15-lb. pressure 10–15 minutes
Reduce pressure slowly
Fixed 7½-lb. pressure 20–30 minutes
Note: Marmalade may also be prepared by the quick method detailed for Ginger Marmalade.

Ginger Marmalade

Makes about 5 lb./2.2 kg.

INGREDIENTS

	Imperial	Metric	American
Seville oranges	3	3	3
Water	1 pt	550 ml.	2½ cups
(If 7½-lb. pressure)	1¼ pt	700 ml.	3 cups
Cooking apples, peeled, cored and grated	1½ lb.	700 kg.	1½ lb.
Sugar	3 lb.	1.4 kg.	3 lb.
Preserved ginger, chopped	4 oz.	100 g.	¼ lb.
Ground ginger	2 tsp.	2 tsp.	2 tsp.

Wash the oranges and place them whole in the pressure cooker with the water (without the trivet). Bring to pressure and cook for given time. Reduce pressure.

Cool sufficiently to cut the peel (but no pith) off the oranges and chop it. Cut the oranges in half, squeeze out the juice and strain it.

Add this, with the orange peel, to the liquor. Tie the pips in a muslin bag and add them to the pressure cooker with the apples. Boil the marmalade for 5 minutes, then remove the muslin bag and discard it. Add the sugar and heat it gently till dissolved. Stir in the preserved ginger and ground ginger. Boil rapidly until setting point is reached (see page 108).

To prevent the peel rising in the jars, cool the marmalade until a skin begins to form on top (about 15 minutes), then pour it into warm, dry jars and cover the tops with wax discs. Cool, cover and label.

COOKING TIME

High/15-lb. pressure 10–15 minutes
Reduce pressure slowly
Fixed 7½-lb. pressure 20–30 minutes

Almond Apricot Jam

✖ Makes 4–5 lb./1.8–2.2 kg.

INGREDIENTS

	Imperial	Metric	American
Dried apricots, washed and cut up	1 lb.	450 g.	1 lb.
Boiling water	2 pt	1 l.	5 cups
(If 7½ lb. pressure)	2¼ pt	1¼ l.	6 cups
Juice 1 lemon			
Sugar	3 lb.	1.4 kg.	3 lb.
Blanched almonds	2 oz.	50 g.	⅓ cup

Put the apricots in the pressure cooker with the boiling water (without the trivet). Cover and leave for 1 hour. Add the lemon juice, bring to pressure and cook for given time. Reduce pressure. Add the sugar and heat gently till it dissolves. Stir in the almonds and boil the jam rapidly in the open pressure cooker until setting point is reached (see page 108). Pour the jam into warm, dry jars and cover the tops with waxed discs. Cool, cover and label.

COOKING TIME
High/15-lb. pressure 10 minutes
Reduce pressure slowly

Fixed 7½-lb. pressure 25 minutes

Apple Jelly

INGREDIENTS

	Imperial	Metric	American
Cooking apples	3 lb.	1.4 kg.	3 lb.
Juice 1 lemon			
Water	1 pt	550 ml.	2½ cups
(If 7½-lb. pressure)	1¼ pt	700 ml.	3 cups
Proportion of sugar to strained juice 1 lb/450 g per	1 pt	550 ml.	2½ cups

Wash the apples, removing any bruised parts, and cut them into thick slices (but do not peel or core them). Place the apples in the pressure cooker with the lemon juice and water (without the trivet). Bring to pressure and cook for given time. Reduce pressure.

Mash the apples and strain them through a jelly bag or double layer of cloth (such as a tea towel or sheeting). Measure the strained juice and put it back into the pressure cooker with the correct amount of sugar. Heat it gently until the sugar dissolves, then boil it rapidly in the open pressure cooker until setting point is reached (see page 108). Pour into warm, dry jars and cover the tops with wax discs. Cool, cover and label.

COOKING TIME
High/15-lb. pressure 3 minutes
Reduce pressure slowly
Fixed 7½-lb. pressure 8 minutes

CHECKPOINT
If the juice is allowed to drop through the jelly bag or cloth, the result will be clearer than if it is forced through.

Redcurrant Jelly

As for apple jelly, using 3 lb./1.4 kg. red currants with $\frac{1}{2}$ pt/300 ml./$1\frac{1}{4}$ cups water ($\frac{3}{4}$ pt/400 ml./2 cups if fixed $7\frac{1}{2}$-lb. pressure). To each 1 pt/550 ml./$2\frac{1}{2}$ cups strained juice add $1\frac{1}{4}$ lb./600 g. sugar.

Blackcurrant Jelly

As for apple jelly, using 3 lb./1.4 kg. black currants with $1\frac{3}{4}$ pt/1 l./$4\frac{1}{2}$ cups water (2 pt/1.1 l./5 cups if fixed $7\frac{1}{2}$-lb. pressure). To each 1 pt/550 ml./$2\frac{1}{2}$ cups strained juice add 1 lb./450 g. sugar.

BOTTLING

Bottling fruit is a simple and attractive way of preserving fresh, ripe summer produce. Nothing gives the cook or the family more pleasure than being able to eat juicy fruits in the middle of winter. Fruit bottling is considerably speeded up if you use your pressure cooker.

CHECKPOINTS FOR BOTTLING FRUIT

The trivet should be used for bottling.

Remember to add to the pressure cooker at least the minimum amount of water recommended by your manufacturer. Check the instruction book for your particular pressure cooker.

Choose bottles which will fit easily into the pressure cooker. When stood on the trivet, they should not touch each other or the sides or lid of the pressure cooker.

Make sure the bottling jars are not damaged in any way. The rubber rings must be flexible and fit the neck of the jar snugly.

Fruits should be ripe, firm and unblemished. Choose fruits of similar size and ripeness.

Fruit can be bottled in water, but a better result is obtained if a syrup is used. To make syrup:

Light syrup: suitable for fruit to be used for tarts, crumbles etc. Boil 2–4 oz./50–100 g./4–8 tbsp. sugar in each 1 pt/550 ml./2½ cups water.

Heavy syrup: suitable for fruit to be used straight as a dessert or for soft fruits which are liable to float in the jar. Boil 6–8 oz./175–225 g./¾–1 cup sugar in each 1 pt/550 ml./2½ cups water.

TO BOTTLE FRUIT

Wash and rinse the jars and lids. Stand them in boiling water till ready to use.

Wash the fruit and prepare according to kind. Pack it firmly into the jars to the shoulder.

Pour boiling syrup over the fruit, leaving ¼ in./½ cm. headspace. To eliminate air bubbles, pour in a little syrup at a time, tapping the jar gently after each addition.

Fit rubber band and tops on the jars. With metal screw bands, screw on till tight, then unscrew turn. Jars with metal clips should be sealed.

Place the trivet in the pressure cooker with boiling water (check with instruction book for correct amount, usually about 2 pt/1 l./5 cups. Stand the jars on the trivet.

Bring to pressure on medium heat and cook for given time (see chart below). Reduce pressure slowly. Pressure cookers with fixed 7½-lb. pressure should be left for 10 minutes before opening.

Fruit	Cooking time at Medium/10-lb. pressure or 7½-lb. pressure
Apples, quarters, thick slices	1 minute
Apricots, whole	1 minute
Blackberries	1 minute
Black currants, Red currants	1 minute
Cherries, whole	1 minute
Damsons, Greengages, Plums, whole	1 minute
Gooseberries	1 minute
Peaches, skinned halves	3 minutes
Pears, peeled, cored and halved	3 minutes
Raspberries	1 minute
Rhubarb	1 minute
Strawberries	3 minutes
Tomatoes, skinned, whole	3 minutes

WEIGHTS AND MEASURES

Ingredients used in the recipes are given in Imperial, Metric and American measures. Generally speaking, the metric and American measures are not exact equivalents of their imperial counterparts. I find it better to work in quantities which have been rounded off to convenient measures. Where I have felt it important to be accurate, exact equivalents are given. It is wise to follow one set of measures throughout a recipe; do not skip from one set to another.

All spoon and cup measures are level unless otherwise stated.

The imperial pint measures 20 fl. oz.; the American pint measures 16 fl. oz.

When cans of food are included in a recipe, the weights given on the label are quoted – these are usually exact equivalents.

When converting your own recipes from imperial to metric quantities, or vice versa, use the tables below as guidelines.

CAPACITY

Imperial	Metric
$\frac{1}{4}$ pt (5 fl. oz.)	150 ml.
$\frac{1}{2}$ pt (10 fl. oz.)	300 ml.
$\frac{3}{4}$ pt (15 fl. oz.)	400 ml.
1 pt (20 fl. oz.)	500–600 ml.
$1\frac{1}{2}$ pt	900 ml.
$1\frac{3}{4}$ pt	1 l.
2 pt	1.1 l.

WEIGHT

Imperial	Metric
1 oz.	25 g.
2 oz.	50 g.
3 oz.	75 g.
4 oz.	100–125 g.
5 oz.	150 g.
6 oz.	175 g.
8 oz.	225 g.
10 oz.	275 g.
12 oz.	350 g.
14 oz.	400 g.
16 oz. (1 lb.)	450 g.
$1\frac{1}{2}$ lb.	700 g.
2 lb.	900 g.
3 lb.	1.4 kg.

QUANTITIES

Most of the recipes in this book are for four people. Some are for six or occasionally more.

These quantities may be halved or quartered as long as the minimum amount of liquid recommended in your instruction book is included. Remember that the amount of liquid used depends on the cooking time and on the size of your pressure cooker, and *not* on the amount of food being cooked.

When doubling up on quantities, check the appropriate section of the book to see how full the pressure cooker should be.

INDEX

Advantages of Pressure Cooking   Page 12
ALL-IN-ONE-MEALS
   Bacon Pilaff   99
   Beef Curry   98
   Boiled Beef and Dumplings   97
   Chicken Risotto   99
   Kedgeree   101
   Old Fashioned Beef Casserole   101
   Vegetable Hotpot   100
Almond Apricot Jam   112
Apricot Condé   84
Apple and Date Dessert   94
Apple Chutney   109
Apple Jelly   112
Apple Sole   70

Bacon Casserole with Dumplings   30
Bacon in Red Wine   31
Bacon Pilaff   99
Banana and Prune Bake   87
Barbecued Beef and Noodles   35
Beans—Chilli   107
Beef Bourguignon   103
Beef Curry   98
Beef in Brown Ale with Cheesy Topping   32
Beef Goulash   35
Beef Pot Roast   37
Blackcurrant Jelly   113
Boiled Beef and Dumplings   97
Bolognese Sauce   37
Bottling   114
Bread and Butter Pudding   95

CASSEROLE
   Bacon with Dumplings   30

Duckling   Page 58
Mustard Rabbit   60
Cauliflower Nicoise   80
Celery in Tomato Sauce   77
Celery Soup   17
Checkpoints for Meats   27
Cheese and Apple Stuffed Mackerel   66
Cherried Chicken   55
Chicken Italienne   54
Chicken—Lemon   53
Chicken Risotto   99
Chicken Treat   51
Chicken with Herbs   54
Chilli Beans   107
Chilli Kidneys   31
Chocolate Pudding   91
Chutney—Apple   109
Christmas Pudding   99
Cock-a-leekie   23
Cod Country Style   68
Cream of Cauliflower Soup   18
Cream of Mushroom Soup   20
Creamy Chicken Casserole   55
Crème Brûlée   104
Crème Caramel   86
Curried Chicken with Sweetcorn   51
Curry—Beef   98
Custard—Egg   86
Cyprus Chicken   52

Date Pudding   84
DESSERTS
   Apple and Date Dessert   94
   Apricot Condé   84
   Banana and Prune Bake   87
   Bread and Butter Pudding   95
   Chocolate Pudding   91
   Christmas Pudding   93
   Crème Caramel   86

Date Pudding	Page	84
Egg Custard		86
Fruit Hat		90
Fruity Pudding		91
Lemon Apricots		89
Peaches in Vanilla Sauce		85
Quick-Baked Apples		94
Raspberry Cream		92
Somerset Pears		95
Spiced Fruit Pudding		89
Vanilla Rice Pudding		87
Devon Haddock		64
Dinner for 4		102
Duck in Pineapple		58
Duckling Casserole		58
Duck with Almonds		105

Egg Custard	86
ENTERTAINING	
Dinner for 4	
Pork and Bacon Pâté	103
Beef Bourguignon	103
Crème Brûlée	104
Lunch or Dinner for 6	
Vichyssoise	105
Duck with Almonds	105
Pears in Red Wine	106
Supper for 8	
Chilli Beans	107
Peach Compote	107

Farmhouse Pâté	24
FISH	
Apple Sole	70
Cheese and Apple Stuffed Mackerel	66

Cod Country Style	Page	68
Devon Haddock		64
Haddock in Creole Sauce		68
Piquant Plaice		65
Plaice Parcels		65
Smoked Haddock Casserole		67
Soused Herrings		69
Tuna Fish		69
Waitaki Fish Scallops		63
French Onion Soup		19
Fruit Hat		70
Fruity Pudding		91

Ginger Marmalade	111
Green Tomato Chutney	110

Haddock—Devon	64
Haddock in Creole Sauce	68
How to care for your Pressure Cooker	11
How to use your Pressure Cooker	7

Jam—Almond Apricot	112
Jelly—Apple	112
Blackcurrant	113
Redcurrant	113

Kedgeree	101
Kidneys—Chilli	31

Lamb Cutlets Italian Style	41
Lemon Apricots	88
Lemon Chicken	53
Lemon Curd	110
Lemon Pork	45
Lentil and Carrot Soup	18

118

Lunch or Dinner for 6 — Page 104

Mackerel—Cheese and Apple Stuffed — 66

MEAT
Bacon Casserole with Dumplings — 30
Bacon in Red Wine — 31
Barbecued Beef and Noodles — 38
Beef Goulash — 35
Beef in Brown Ale with Cheesy Topping — 32
Beef Hot Roast — 37
Bolognese Sauce — 37
Chilli Kidneys — 31
Lamb Cutlets Italian Style — 41
Lemon Pork — 45
Paprika Lamb Cutlets — 39
Pepperpot Beef — 39
Pineapple Bacon — 29
Pork Chops with Apple Sauce — 46
Pork Stroganoff — 45
Redcurrant Lamb Roll — 42
Rich Lamb Casserole — 41
Sherry Bacon — 28
Somerset Pork — 44
Steak and Kidney Pudding — 33
Thrifty Beef Roll — 36
Traditional Lamb Hot Pot — 43
Veal and Mushroom Cream — 47
Veal Roll with Herbs — 48
Minestrone — 22
Minty Lamb Rolls — 40
Mustard Rabbit Casserole — 60

Old Fashioned Beef Casserole — 101
Onion Butter Beans — 80
Orange Marmalade — 111
Oxtail Soup — 21

Paprika Lamb Cutlets — 39
Peach Compote — 107
Peaches in Vanilla Sauce — 85

Pears in Red Wine — Page 106
Pepperpot Beef — 34
Pheasant with Apple Cream — 59
Pigeon Ragout — 59
Pilaff—Bacon — 99
Pineapple Bacon — 29
Piquant Plaice — 65
Plaice Parcels — 65
Pork and Bacon Pâté — 103
Pork Chops with Apple Sauce — 46
Pork Stroganoff — 45
Potato and Mint Soup — 22
Potato Pie — 77
Potage Darblay — 20

POULTRY AND GAME — 50
Cherried Chicken — 55
Chicken Italienne — 54
Chicken Treat — 51
Chicken with Herbs — 54
Creamy Chicken Casserole — 55
Curried Chicken with Sweetcorn — 51
Cyprus Chicken — 52
Duck in Pineapple — 58
Duckling Casserole — 58
Lemon Chicken — 53
Mustard Rabbit Casserole — 60
Pheasant with Apple Cream — 59
Pigeon Ragout — 59
Rabbit in Orange — 60
Turkey in Apple Juice — 57
Turkey Marengo — 56

PRESERVES — 108
Almond Apricot Jam — 112
Apple Chutney — 109
Apple Jelly — 112
Blackcurrant Jelly — 113
Ginger Marmalade — 111
Green Tomato Chutney — 110
Lemon Curd — 110
Orange Marmalade — 111

Redcurrant Jelly	Page 113	
Rhubarb Chutney	109	
Quick Baked Apples	94	
Rabbit in Orange	60	
Raspberry Cream	92	
Ratatouille	74	
Redcurrant Jelly	113	
Redcurrant Lamb Roll	42	
Rhubarb Chutney	109	
Rich Lamb Casserole	41	
Safety Note	10	
Sauce—Bolognese	37	
Savoury Starters	24	
Savoury Stuffed Tomatoes	79	
Sherry Bacon	28	
Smoked Haddock Casserole	67	
Somerset Pears	95	
Somerset Pork	44	

SOUPS AND STARTERS

Celery Soup	17
Cock-a-Leekie	23
Cream of Cauliflower Soup	18
Cream of Mushroom Soup	20
Farmhouse Pâté	24
French Onion Soup	19
Lentil and Carrot Soup	18
Minestrone	22
Oxtail Soup	21
Potage Darblay	20
Potato and Mint Soup	22
Savoury Starters	24
Stock	16
Thick Country Vegetable Soup	17
Thick Pea Soup	23
Tomato Soup	19
Soused Herring	69
Spiced Cabbage	76

Spiced Fruit Pudding	Page 89
Spicy Stuffed Onions	78
Steak and Kidney Pudding	33
Stock	16
Stuffed Peppers	75
Stuffed Cabbage	76
Supper for 8	106
Thick Country Vegetable Soup	17
Thick Pea Soup	23
Thrifty Beef Roll	36
Tomato Soup	19
Traditional Lamb Hot Pot	43
Tuna Fish	69
Turkey in Apple Juice	59
Turkey Marengo	56
Vanilla Rice Pudding	87
Veal Roll with Herbs	48
Veal and Mushroom Cream	47

VEGETABLES

Cauliflower Niçoise	80
Celery in Tomato Sauce	77
Onion Butter Beans	80
Potato Pie	77
Ratatouille	74
Savoury Stuffed Tomatoes	79
Spiced Cabbage	76
Spicy Stuffed Onions	78
Stuffed Cabbage	76
Stuffed Peppers	75
Vegetable Hotpot	100
Vichyssoise	105

What about your Pressure Cooker	12
What you get	13
Waitaki Fish Scallops	63
Your Pressure Cooker and your Freezer	11